Messages From A Sent One

Douglas Montague

ISBN (Paperback): 979-8-9884655-7-7
ISBN (Hardcover): 979-8-9885619-3-4
ISBN (eBook): 979-8-9884655-6-0

FORWARD

Douglas is a true student of the Word. He devours, digests, and delights in the Scriptures, then can apply what he's learned to everyday life situations with uncanny ability. This book will not only be engrossing, it will be a reference book you will go to again and again.

Faith Adkins Brasel
Friend, Coworker in the Kingdom, and President of Omega World Missions
Ellettsville, Indiana

- - - -

I have known Douglas since college days long ago. He wrote a play one of our first years there and we performed it at a local Mayfest for the public. I still have that copy — The Woman at the Well. I cherish it because the words that God puts in Douglas' mouth to share with the Body of Christ are powerful and penetrating in their simplicity. The stories are real and pertinent. You will not be able to put down this book because of the fascinating and real to life stories he shares. They all have a deeper message from the heart of our Father which makes them important and not trivial. I heartily recommend this book from the pen of my dear friend.

Jenifer Mahler
Founder, Hearts Triumphant

- - - -

I am so glad that Rev. Douglas has produced a book. He writes with much clarity and with much God-given wisdom. Above all, he leads us to God's truth. Through his writings, he helps us understand, live, and experience God's truth.

Andrew Yeoh
Penang, Malaysia

- - - -

Doug has devoted his life to serving the Lord in every way he can. God has blessed him with an uncanny ability to see the connection between everyday events and the wisdom of the scriptures! Such insights shine a light for others to find Jesus!

Mark Sidebottom
Versailles Missouri

- - - -

Douglas is a well-known Bible teacher.

He is constantly contacted by many church leaders for advice. Douglas sees the Bible as God's word and manual for successful, victorious living. He consistently refers all those who seek his guidance to the Bible as the answer to all problems.

Pastor Tony Tan
Creation Community International AG
Klang, Malaysia

- - - -

Inspiring, heart touching, and life transforming messages from the missionary who brings biblical truth to daily life's situations for many ministers of God as well as ordinary people, mostly based on the questions of those people. This book will help people to get answers for their questions but above everything else, will help everyone to get closer to God and to love His Word, the Bible.

Roman Vretonko
Pastor, Teacher, Church Planter
Czech Republic

- - - -

The Lord has blessed me to know Douglas and receive divine guidance through him for many years. I'm excited that many others will have the opportunity to be equally blessed by this man who has an amazing heart and love for the Lord!

Mike Blackmon
Devoted Follower of Christ
Broken Arrow, Oklahoma

- - - -

From the time I met Douglas when our youngest sons were in school, I have been impressed by his unwavering commitment to God and His Word. Rarely have I met someone who is truly a student of the Word. His passion for the Word transcends into his passion to train Church leaders. Douglas' teaching will challenge you to become a student of the Word too. Accept that challenge and you will become closer to and more like Jesus.

Chris Anderson
friend and student of the Word
Catoosa, Oklahoma

- - - -

I have learned much from Douglas's newsletters and articles over the years. They are unique and practical for the layman, the student, or the pastor.

Pastor Al Rennert
Lovington, Illinois

- - - -

My life has been very blessed by meeting Pastor Douglas who was on a mission trip in the north zone of Costa Rica. He was used to visiting tropical places in his missions travels. His articles have always encouraged me. His sermons make me think a lot. From modern topics to deep end-of-times analysis, plus current events, he always knows how to present God's words in the best way possible, using more than just English. Philosophical, theological, and even practical teachings plus occasional jokes, but he always maintains a deep understanding of the Kingdom of God. It has always been my pleasure to read what God has given pastor Douglas. I know God will speak to your heart when you read the messages in this book. God bless you!

Andrés Joseph Jiménez Leandro
Light Squadron of the Trumpet Call International Ministries
San Carlos, Alajuela, Costa Rica

- - - -

I have known Pastor Douglas for more than twenty years since I was a youth. His experiences as an on-field servant and an avid student of the Bible have inspired me to follow his godly example as a servant of the Lord. The collection of his messages are biblically grounded and ministerially applicable. It is easy to read and yet thought provoking in thinking through contemporary issues that are happening now. It is definitely worthwhile to spend time reading through this book.

Alex Wan
Cross cultural missionary
S.E. Asia

- - - -

You're about to read words of wisdom from a man rich in ministry over much of the world, who has gained his knowledge by thousands of hours in God's Word. He has lived a life of faith, trusting God when there was no help but God. He loves the church and it's pastors. His counsel to young or new missionaries is not to be missed.

Fred L.
Elder Emeritus
Allen, Texas

- - - -

The writings contained in this book are not the ivory tower musings of one detached from the fray. These chapters are born out of spiritual boot camp and spiritual campaign battlefield. They are penned by one who is equipped and experienced to edify and equip the younger as well as challenge, edify and encourage the older. The soundness and integrity of the author are tried and true. This wit and wisdom in this book deserves to be read, absorbed, and implemented.

Benjamin W. Waters
Elder, Covenant Life Fellowship
Lubbock, Texas

- - - -

I have come to know Pastor Douglas through the many years of his impactful ministry. I am confident that as you flip through the pages of this book, you will be empowered in your personal walk with Christ through his countless experiences in the mission field. Douglas has a way of capturing the reader with his wit and humour, and his impeccable ability to take the most complex thoughts and questions and communicate them in a way that helps any reader understand from the get go.

The pages of this book are filled with honest reflections of his journey - including the highs and the lows, yet you will come to discover his rock solid, never-wavering, firmly-footed faith in his God. I pray this book encourages you, the way it did for me.

Kuilan Suppiah
Senior Pastor
Trinity Baptist Church
Alor Setar, Malaysia

- - - -

Missionary Montague has preached and taught in our church a few times. With humor, knowledge, and wisdom, he can draw from a sea of lessons, mostly by memory, that catch our attention.

Pastor Silva
Las Olas Worship Center
Fort Lauderdale, Florida

- - - -

Brother Douglas is a humble servant who helps us with simple teaching from God's Word. He fellowships easily with pastors who are scattered in many villages. He encourages and helps motivate those who are pioneering new churches. He leads seminars for blessing God's servants from many kinds of denominations so that they will seek to have Christlike qualities in their character.

I have known him for more than 30 years. I am very blessed by his easy to understand teaching. Pastors from many backgrounds here in North Sumatra are grateful for brother Douglas' teaching ministry.

Pastor Simon Petrus Ginting
Foursquare Gospel Church
Village of Kuta Mbaru
Sumatra, Indonesia

- - - -

Your stories have been very insightful from your missionary perspective. I have appreciated your shepherd's heart in your letters of exhortation and have often gleaned good wisdom, and instruction from them.

Sharon Justice
Chaplain/Director
Preparing Messiah's Inheritance International
Fort Worth, Texas

- - - -

Brother Douglas is my faithful friend. He is a servant of Christ Jesus. He walks with a diligent faith. When I read his updates from remote areas of North Sumatra where he travels for weeks with his lovely wife Ruth, or when they come serve in our region, I am amazed by their faithfulness. This helps to inspire me and my family to move on in our service for our Lord in whatever way we can. All glory to the Lord! May the Lord bless them both.

Marianne Balang
Secretary of Prayer Team, Limbang District
Borneo Evangelical Ministry
Limbang, E. Malaysia

- - - -

As Douglas interacts with his inquirers, his readers will quickly sense that his replies represent the product of his life-long practice of daily immersion in the sacred text. Douglas' intense, daily, personal Scriptural study becomes exhibit A as the dynamic truth that the God-breathed Scriptures are indeed "profitable for teaching, for reproof, for correction, and for training in righteousness" (2 Tim. 3:16) comes leaping to life in these wonderful interactions. Readers will find spiritual "soul-food" for the betterment of their inner person.

Jack Van Vessem
Retired after 40 years of service with several national and international ministries
Garland, Texas

- - - -

Douglas Montague has been serving the Lord in His fields for many years now and has stayed focused on his task of strengthening the Church in several quadrants of this world by teaching the Word of God clearly to as many as God gives him to serve. This compilation of some of his recent teachings are insightful and helpful to the Church whether in remote islands or in cities overseas as well as in the United States. You will be blessed.

Karl Bunjes
College roommate of Douglas and retired pastor
Blanco, Texas

Acknowledgements

There was a reason why I was not in church on Sunday the 17th of July in 1955. My father was serving in his first full time ministry in a small church in Woodville, Mississippi when Mom became pregnant with me in the fall of 1954.

As the family story goes, the doctor who would eventually deliver me into this world was befuddled as to when to predict my appearance to happen. He told them that event would take place by the end of May or in early June. He was off by 6 weeks.

When Mom did finally go into labor on Saturday the 16th of July, Dad carried her 14 miles over to Centreville since that town had a hospital. The doctor was convinced that things were progressing very slowly, which was typical of first-born children.

So he assured my Dad that I would not be forthcoming from the womb until late night on Sunday or beyond. He knew that my Dad's biggest day of the week was Sunday. He told him,

“Just go home tonight, have a good rest, then after you fulfill all your Sunday morning duties, you can come back tomorrow after lunch to await the big event.”

That is exactly what my Dad did. After his Sunday lunch, he collected up a pile of magazines and newspapers to be prepared for a long time to spend in the hospital waiting room. But to his surprise, his first born son had managed to throw everyone another curve ball, and before noon, I had made it out of the birth canal.

In other words, I was born while my Dad was in the middle of his Sunday morning sermon. That is why I was not in church that day.

After that, you can be assured that Douglas was raised in church. That fact also describes both my Dad and my Mom’s background. I come from a family of church goers.

Fast forward to the end of my Freshman year in college. Coming up soon on my 19th birthday, the Lord began to call me. He asked me to become His servant. But I had fallen in love with aviation since I was 11 years old, and dreamed of a career in which I could fly for a living. So frankly I was shocked by the idea that the Lord had a different plan in mind for my life.

When I realized that the Lord would not change His mind about calling me into His service, I reluctantly consented and surrendered. For the next 3 years of undergrad work, and then

2 out of 3 years of a seminary program, I thought His call meant becoming a local church pastor like my own Dad had lived out in several different pastorates.

Lo and behold, during my last year of seminary, the Lord twisted the dial on the side of the microscope. To my utter shock, He sharpened the focus to make clear to me that my calling did NOT mean becoming a pastor in America like my Dad. Instead the Lord clarified that my calling was to be a teacher of His Word, and that the first place He would send me to do that was in faraway Indonesia, a place I could barely find on a world map!

Once I committed to prepare for ministry instead of aviation, my Mom told me something. She said she had a feeling about me that "whatever kind of ministry Douglas will someday do, it just won't be a typical ministry."

She and Dad were loving and supportive through all the years that I still had to prepare for a life of service in fields unto the ends of the earth. As that kind of work began in 1986, Dad and Mom were always encouraging to me. I am forever grateful that they did not try to pressure me into a certain mold for how one should be "a minister." Though Dad left this world at age 91 in 2017 and Mom followed in 2022, I still want to dedicate this book to their memory.

TABLE OF CONTENTS

A Poor Pastor?
Why So Poor?

In December of 2021, while Ruth and I served in Costa Rica, my friend Pastor Freddy brought us to downtown San José (the capital) to meet with the leaders of a Chinese flock there. While awaiting their pastor to finish up a meeting, we went to a nearby coffee shop and bumped into another pastor who was from Nicaragua who would soon catch a bus back home. So the four of us ended up in a coffee shop for almost an hour. Since then, that brother from Nicaragua has kept in touch with me via WhatsApp.But this morning, he has put out a plea for offerings to be sent him. Pas. Freddy had already warned me that many Nicaraguan pastors look upon us *gringos de Norte Americana* (white folks from United States) as cash cows to be milked for as much as they can get.So in seeking the Lord on how to respond to him, the following just got composed and sent. I hope you too will be blessed by this exhortation:

- - - -

Solomon says, "Better is a friend who is near than a brother far away" (Prov. 27:10).

When I was briefly your brother **in your presence** in San José earlier this month, I paid for your meal at the coffee shop, and I gave you 10,000 colones (a bit more than $15). That money was not from Pas. Freddy but from me.

Now I am in transit back to Asia, with many extra expenses that have come up while having unexpected delays that cause us to spend an extra week in California before we should board our flights to Malaysia this Friday.

So your help needs to arise from a friend who is near at this point than seeking help from a brother far away, according to His counsel.

And when you say that you are poor, maybe that is truly your situation. But what is the Lord's solution for His people so that they have sufficient wages?

It is found in a couple of places. First, consider this short statement: "The laborer is worthy of his wages" (1 Tim. 5:18).

Un obrero es digno para su salario. No un mendigo, pero solo un obrero (not "a beggar is worthy of wages.")

Another truth to review: "Let him who is **taught the Word** share all good things with him **who teaches His Word**" (Gal. 6:6).

So since I hardly know you very well, I just ask you to check yourself with these truths that affect your overall financial welfare.

Are you a worker for the Lord? I did not ask if you hold a title as a pastor or some other kind of laborer called into the service of our Lord Jesus. Unfortunately, there are many in Christendom who call themselves "servants of the Lord," but in reality, they are lazy and not truly doing the works which He has called them to do. So if you are not using the strength of body and the clarity of mind each day that Jesus already gives you to apply yourself to your earthly duties that are directed by Heaven, then why should you expect any wages sufficient unto your needs?

Secondly, **teaching His Word** truly is a task that requires diligence in spending significant time **daily** in two things: You need to be…

In His Word, while…

In His presence.

Pharisees were known to do the first item but failed to do so while fulfilling the second.

Modern-day charismatics are known for chasing the second item while neglecting the first item.

But if you, my brother, do both, I can assure you that He who is known by many names and titles in the Scriptures, including the one called **the Word**, He will surely teach you many things. Then you will be equipped to turn to your flock and to really teach them what their minds need in order to leave behind immaturity and become adults in the Lord.

Only spiritual adults become givers and tithers, not babes in Christ. Help your flock to grow by, first, you repenting of using your pulpit time to just jump up and down and scream over and over the same few things you have already declared to them. It hasn't worked, and it obviously hasn't been blessed by Heaven, or else you would not be in this poor situation. No, you must by His grace and wisdom begin to fulfill your duty to actually **teach His Word**.

And then, when you do so, the impact upon those in front of you who do have some maturity in the Lord will say to themselves, "Wow! This servant really blessed my mind and heart today with God's Word explained so well. I should do something for him to show my gratitude in a tangible way." That's when they take you out to lunch and pay for it. That's when they become regular tithers. That's when real adults in the Lord give you occasional extra offerings, whether of money or of things that your family needs.

What I am presenting here to you, my brother, is what He showed me **to do** many years ago. Since then, I have been walking out these bits of His wisdom, and He has met our needs all along our way.

¡Dios te bendiga, mi hermano en Cristo!

(Translation: God bless you, my brother in Christ!)

- - - -

Decisions Prompted by Fear or His Spirit?

A Czech brother whom I met in His fields laboring in the Philippines when I too was there a few years ago just gave me an update on what's going on among the saints in Europe.

He described how often the rules keep changing by those governments in regard to allowing or forbidding travel inside the EU due to Covid developments. I replied with, "Folks just need to *calm down*. We are not all going to die from this thing! The Lord won't let that happen."

He wrote, "I know, I know. This is not the end of the world yet. The worst thing is that Covid in many churches divides people. So sad."

At that point, the following arose from my thoughts, and I hope you too will be blessed and edified:

- - - -

Ahh, what you are describing, I have given it a name, and among English speakers, I don't usually have to explain it very much after they hear it the first time I say it. It is called *fleshoship*.

We divide ourselves along lines where we hold the same opinions, and with those who agree with me, I enjoy fleshoship, but with those who do not, I avoid them, even though many of them are actually my brethren in Christ Jesus.

So we have allowed ourselves to create new sects within His body, as in those who listen to and thoroughly agree with all government pronouncements and restrictions in regard to this virus problem and those who remain skeptical of all governmental declarations and edicts. I imagine we could yet see new churches forming that have their origins when they were all together in one flock, with the new one calling themselves the "First Church of the Masked and Socially Distant," and the church they left now calling themselves the "First Church of the Unveiled Faces."

This is a sad state of affairs. How did some of us reach this point? Because of decisions reached that were based upon fear. Can anyone show me a biblical example where at the crossroads to make a choice, when that choice was made out of fear, the consequences thereafter were good?

Before Moses was born, what decision was made by the pharoah of Egypt concerning what should be done about the growing population of Hebrews in their midst? Based on a speculative fear that maybe someday, the Hebrews would choose to ally themselves with an enemy of Egypt, the then-pharaoh decided to oppress and persecute the Hebrews to the point of ordering the murder of Hebrew baby boys.

How did that decision based upon fear turn out for the empire of Egypt? They set themselves up as the enemy of God Almighty, and when God chose to take action, Egypt was completely destroyed!

Gideon is celebrated as a great and godly warrior against the menacing power of neighboring Midian who had brought the Hebrews much harassment and deprivation. But before the Lord could begin to use Gideon in a mighty way, what did He have to do in Gideon's life? He had to get Gideon to stop making decisions based upon his fears and instead get him to trust in the guidance of the Lord. Read it for yourself in just two chapters, Judges 6 and 7.

What happened to Caiaphas and to those who sided with him when he pronounced, "It is expedient for you that better is the death of one man than that the whole nation should perish"? It was their fear of Jesus and His growing popularity and influence that was the basis of their decision to seek how to get Jesus destroyed.

When they cried out to Pilate, "His blood be upon us and our children, for we have no king but Caesar," what was the outcome for their nation? The Jews rose up in rebellion against Rome in 66 AD, and across the next four years, the Romans crushed them entirely, including those atop Masada, the temple was torn down, and any Jewish survivors were scattered throughout the empire, sold into slavery.

In more recent history, when Prime Minister Neville Chamberlain and other European leaders saw the rise of Adolph Hitler and the Nazis, in their fear of him, what decision did they make? They chose the path of appeasement, thinking Herr Hitler would calm down and be peaceable once all the Germanic people were under the Nazi flag. How did that choice based upon their fear of Hitler turn out? Ever since, we call those years in 1939–1945 the horrific event of World War II, in which millions died and more suffered terribly.

We all make decisions. But what is it that prompts and guides the choices we make? If it is various fears that seem altogether reasonable, yet fear is fear, and we see it is a bad start to good decision-making.

But the godly man or woman has the advantage of listening to the voice of the Lord and then going forward in a certain direction based upon faith in Him and in His goodness and in His wisdom. Look at the contrast between the decisions of Saul's army facing the giant for forty days and the choice of David once he saw and heard the challenge of Goliath just once? Saul's army were afraid and thus ran away and did not bring relief or glory to their king. David was led by the Lord to go forward (even though Saul and the other Hebrews thought that this did not make sense), so fearless David ran to meet the giant in battle, and through him the Lord brought great victory that was enjoyed by the entire kingdom.

We must consider these things carefully and Scripturally. Decision-making based upon one or more fears always ends badly. But making choices that are guided by His Spirit will be blessed by Heaven.

I still recall something that happened to me during the initial two years of getting the original support base together that would enable me and my family to relocate from America to begin work as a cross-cultural servant on the other side of the globe. With sad faces, one couple communicated to me why they could not justify becoming part of that support base. They said that from what they had heard of daily life over there, there were just too many dangers that might even threaten or hurt the welfare of my young children.

I recall writing back to them to say that I did not believe that God's leading to become a missionary meant that He loved me or my children less than if we remained inside our homeland. Indeed, the support base that He raised up for my family was from those who were unafraid to become senders of a goer family. And across those years, the Lord proved He could and would provide for my children in every way.The unafraid led by His Spirit always makes better choices than do the fearful. Always!

- - - -

My Willpower or His Perseverance?

After a sister read the things that our family is now dealing with, she wrote back that she admired my perseverance in the face of these difficulties. But I thought something needed to be clarified so that Jesus gets more credit than me for the peace that we still hold even while these Visa matters remain unresolved. Here's what I replied, and I hope you too are blessed and edified:

- - - -

According to John, there are three things in Jesus:

1. Tribulation

2. Kingdom

3. Perseverance

(Rev. 1:9)

If we His people will just continue to lean upon the living Lord Jesus, in Him is sufficient perseverance for *all* that we face and deal with. It's not like I need folks to admire my willpower to stay in His program. There is too much teaching from pulpits, in my opinion, that keeps urging the saints to stay strong and to say, "You can do it!"

It is not our willpower that is more precious than gold to our Lord. Rather it is our faith in Him while under pressure or duress that is more precious than gold to Him, according to 1 Pet. 1:6 and 7.

And I might add this:

No one likes tribulation things.

But everyone likes Kingdom things.

So how do you make the transition from the first thing to the next thing, from tribulation stuff to Kingdom stuff? That's where His third thing kicks in, which is **His perseverance**.

It could be said that Joshua and Caleb leaned upon the Lord for perseverance, and those two men did indeed end up in the Promised Land as both conquerors and inheritors of many blessings. But the majority of their cohorts who also got out of Egypt ended up with their corpses buried out in the dry and desolate wilderness.

As Moses said in Deut. 6:23, "The Lord brought us out to bring us in." Sounds good, but those who wouldn't trust Him for perseverance never got that second part of being brought in.

So as I often ask folks when teaching on this subject, "Where would you like to die?", you should see their puzzled facial expressions. What kind of question is that?

So I must clarify that for believers, there's only one of two places for us to die: You can barely come into salvation but then resist His sanctifying work so that you too will die in the wilderness or you can let Him keep working on you so that you are ready to become a soldier instead of a whiny, complaining rebel against all authority, and then you will be ready for Him to bring you into the Promised Land full of blessings to enjoy before you die.

So where do you wanna die—in the wilderness or the Promised Land? His perseverance in one's life (or lack thereof) will determine where one's corpse will eventually be buried.

- - - -

He Is the Waymaker!

Are you familiar with the worship song titled "Waymaker"? When Ruth and I served one week at a Christian camp in the summer of 2020, that song was a favorite which was repeated many times.

I think it is much more than a lovely song—it is the truth, blunt and straight as an arrow. Our Lord knows how to make a way for His people, no matter what is currently our lot or what is just around the corner that will shock and stun the worldly crowd around us.

What if you were Noah and the Lord told you that He was about to flood the entire earth and everything that you were already familiar with would be wiped out and washed away? I think his heart would tremble while waiting for what else He would say next.

And then he heard instructions on what the Lord wanted him to do before that flood comes. "Build an ark." *Say, what?*

Build... what? But I don't know how to do that. "Make it this long and this high and that wide..."

If anyone else had told you that there is a way to be kept safe from a world-wide flood, you just wouldn't believe your ears. But if the Lord tells you that there is a way to be saved from all of the death and destruction that would come at His command, you would have to remind yourself, "Then my salvation *must* be possible." And Noah got busy according to His counsel, and after a hundred years, that ark was indeed ready and capable to keep him and his family safe from the horrors of judgment that were imminently coming upon such a corrupt earth.

And yet at times, I let myself think I have it tough to rely upon Him and His solution for Andrew and for us two. If He could manage to keep Noah safe, then certainly I can relax about what concerns us three nowadays.

- - - -

Biblical Perspective on Slavery

A pastor friend in Malaysia reached me with a query asking, "Does God condone slavery?" He said this topic was brought up by a church member. Here's what the pastor sent me:

"God didn't create slaves. Man did. Does God condone slavery? Christ requires us to love our neighbors and even our enemies, so how can a Christian truly be a genuine Christian if he is inhumane to his fellow man?

Slavery is referred to many times in the Bible by St. Paul and is not condemned, but the relationship between slaves and masters is regulated. Slaves are to respect the master who is to treat them right and fair, as he too has a Master in Heaven."

- - - -

When you consider who to blame for slavery, I would put it squarely upon Satan. Slavery by definition means that one has no freedom of choice because he or she has been enslaved by someone else. Two examples stand out in the Scriptures to support this view.

Who was overpowering that boy who was often rescued from the self-destruction of either throwing himself into deep water to drown or falling into a roaring fire to burn himself up? That was a powerful demon manifesting his control over that boy. And what did Jesus do? Jesus cast that controlling spirit out of the boy to set his will free again (Mark 9:17–27).

The other example is found when Jesus shows up on the shores of Gadara and is met by a wild naked man whose body is covered in dried blood from self-inflicted wounds, who lived only in the local graveyard and who terrified the nearby village with his hellish screams at all hours of the night. Who was forcing that man to live that way? It was a legion of demons. And what did Jesus do? He cast those thousand demons out of the man so that now he was free again to choose to wash off all of that blood, put on clothes, stop hurting himself, and to sit at Jesus' feet in his right mind, calm and peaceful (Mark 5:1–20).

Now I ask, does the Lord have enough power to force me to do or to say anything that He desires? Yes, of course. He is not called the Most High God for nothing.

So could He pull a string in Heaven where the other end is wrapped around my wrist to force me to suddenly raise that hand over my head in a sign of worship of Him? Yes, He could do that. But so far, that's never happened to me.

Instead, I find that I am gently led or urged by His Spirit that sometimes while I am worshipping the Lord, I would like to add that gesture while I am praying or singing unto Him my praises. So, I choose to follow that leading, and I willingly raise my hand or hands as a way to give honor to Him.

So here are two terms: to be a slave or to be a free man. And what two words are associated with each of those men? A slave is controlled, but a free man is to be led.

The Lord could control me, but He doesn't want to. He prefers to lead me. David affirmed this twice in Psalm 23, saying, "He **leads** me beside the still waters" and "He **leads** me in paths of righteousness for His name's sake." Paul added, "All those who are **led by the Spirit of God**, these are the sons of God" (Romans 8:14).

John wrote that Jesus "appeared for this purpose, so that He might destroy the works of the devil" (1 John 3:8). What is the goal of the devil? To see how many people he can put under the bondage of slavery. But as Paul affirmed, "It was for **freedom** that Christ set you free, therefore keep standing firm, and do not submit again to **a yoke of slavery**" (Gal. 5:1).

So this topic of slavery is not just about the overly simple idea of one human owning another person and forcing him or her to obey the slave master's will. Even though Paul did not try to incite among slaves in his day the overthrow of all human slavery, he did admonish slaves saying, "Were you called (i.e., to become a Christian) while a slave? Do not worry about it; but if you are able also to become free, rather do that" (1 Cor. 7:21). And "You were bought with a price; do not become slaves of men" (1 Cor. 7:23).

For Christians, this is about how various kinds of leaders fulfill their roles in relation to those who are called to honor and follow their lead. God has called various folks to fulfill one of the five offices in His churches (Eph. 4:11). He has called each husband to be the head of his wife (Eph. 5:22–33). He has called children to honor and obey their parents (Eph. 6:1–3).

But if a pastor or other church leader exercises that position in a way that tries to dominate and control that flock, that is like unto putting the flock under the yoke of slavery. If the Lord prefers to lead us gently by His Word, His Spirit, and His example, then church leaders should choose to lead the flock in that same way. That's what Peter said (1 Pet. 5:1–4).

Yes, a Christian husband has headship over his wife. But my head doesn't just give orders to my body on what to do 24/7; rather my head is in touch through the God-given nervous system with all parts of my body so that whenever a body part feels weak or injured, that message reaches my brain so that my thoughts can be applied on what to do next to help my whole body to become strong and restored to good health. There is a wonderful unity and harmony that happens daily between my head and all my body parts.

What about Dad and Mom in relation to their children? If Christian masters back in the first century were exhorted (Eph. 6:9) that they needed to give up threatening their slaves (which by definition of the master-slave relationship those masters had every right to do), then how much threatening should godly parents do in fulfilling their task to train up their children in the way that they should go? (Prov. 22:6).

Yes, when the child ranges from an infant to a toddler to a small child, sure, parents must control their lives and their environment to assure them the safety from dangers which they don't yet comprehend around them. But godly parents have the goal of helping their children to see in their example that Dad and Mom seek to be led by the Lord so that their children will want to do likewise as they enter their adolescent years.

Children are not to be slaves but rather to become the Lord's free servants. Thus, Christian parents have a goal to help their children so that when they become young adults and begin making their own decisions in life that those children have experienced the benefits of being raised by their Dad and Mom who sought to be led by His Spirit in all things.

- - - -

The Mess or the Message?

A West Texas brother called me recently. Our chats are not usually about pleasantries concerning sports and weather. We really fellowship around the things of the Lord and what His Word says to us, to His churches, and about what's going on around us in this world.

Something bubbled up from my heart. It had to do with what should be a regular thing going on in His flocks everywhere but, alas, is oftentimes seemingly missing. It's about the message.

You are probably familiar with the gas gauge on the car dashboard. The traditional layout has an "E" on the left end of that scale and an "F" on the right. When the needle gets close to the "E," your tank is almost empty. I once heard that the definition of *pedestrian* is a driver who says "There's still two more gallons in the tank when the needle is on 'E.'"

The closer the tank is to empty, the wise driver has a great sense of urgency to find a gas station soon and fill up. In contrast, there's a great sense of satisfaction when you see the needle pegged to the right of the full indicator.

What if our hearts had a gauge to measure how full or how close to empty we are in relation to the messages that come forth from those who have that responsibility? I have found five passages that could be arranged from the bleakest to the best. Where do you see the gauge needle on your heart after you have attended a Sunday school lesson, or a worship service, or a home fellowship meeting?

So here are the texts for the sliding scale of our responses to the various sermons that saints or sinners hear from today's servants. Let's begin from the "E" end of the gauge and work our way over to the "F" end.

Ecclesiastes 1:1, 2

> The preacher says all is vanity and emptiness. This shows the reader how dry and distant from the Lord Solomon's heart had become in his latter years. That king observed how all the rivers flow to the sea, and yet the sea is never full.
>
> And this is a complaint? So what would happen to all the dry land if one day the sea was full so that the rivers ceased to flow and the rivers were no more? Would the deserts of the world benefit if only they had some rivers running through them? Yet those things which pass for *messages* today can be just as dry and as empty

as was Solomon's heart in his latter years. What came out of Solomon in his senior years was more of a mess than a message.

Matthew 23:2, 3, 15

The Pharisees' messages contained biblical truths. But the lives of the Pharisees contained hypocrisy, thus resulting in their followers becoming twice the sons of hell as themselves. But the Pharisees never really expected the multitudes to respond well to their messages (John 7:49), believing that the masses were cursed to a level of stupidity which made understanding the Law of God unattainable by them. Only good Pharisees could grasp such theology. So the masses found their messages as tedious and condescending at best.

Ezekiel 33:30–33

Even though this prophet is honored as a true and good messenger of the Lord, his hearers only enjoyed the messages. But they did not change and did not become practitioners of those messages. So, the listeners are like the saints that Jesus described as being like the rocky soil. After His Word is sown, they enjoy those messages, but due to the hidden rocks below, no roots can grow, and thus no fruit will ever be produced from those who won't become doers of His Word.

Acts 2:37–41

> After hearing Peter proclaim the gospel message, the hearts of lost souls who heard him were pricked unto repentance, and they gave themselves over to be baptized in Jesus' name. Peter's message was clear and precise, easily understood, and not difficult to act upon immediately by many who heard it.

Luke 24:32

> After hearing Jesus' message as two believers walked with Him, they testified, "Did not our hearts burn within us as Jesus explained to us the Scriptures?" Then they ran back to find His grieving disciples to testify that Jesus was indeed risen from the dead. They were truly filled with a message from on high! How many saints can say that the messages they hear each week cause their hearts to burn within them and now they want to go and share some of that good news with others?

- - - -

In a recent chat with a brother in Oklahoma, again this topic took center stage. Here is the lion's share:

- - - -

Have you noticed that in most, maybe all, of the services you have attended, you have two reactions to what transpires after you have arrived and the service begins?

If the worship leaders and musicians carry out their part in humility instead of showboating, your reaction is one of gratitude for their help to lead you into His presence to give Him much praise and thanksgiving, for which our Lord is entirely worthy. Am I correct?

But once that team finishes their part, the pastor comes to the pulpit. Now what is your reaction to what he brings next? Are you truly taught something and edified by the insights and exhortation that are presented? Or are you either just entertained by his oratory or bored by his lack of appeal to your emotions? Worse, are you left feeling judged and/or condemned by lots of do's and don'ts which are designed to elicit your sense of guilt for failing the Lord in this way or that?

\- - - -

Oklahoma brother: "With our pastor, I am consistently blessed by his message, and it reaffirms that the Lord speaks through him."

\- - - -

Then you have used the very word that I am longing for, either when I am on deck to be in the pulpit or when I am not on deck but rather sitting in front of any pulpit during a service, and that is the word *message*.

Malachi refers to God's servants as **messengers of the Lord of hosts** (Mal. 2:7).

I have taught groups of pastors using this text. While in the middle of a seminar where I am teaching, if the main door to that venue suddenly banged open and a young man breathlessly comes running inside toward us, crying out, "I am a messenger, I am a messenger!" what would be our reaction? We would say, "Ok, ok, catch your breath, and then tell us, what is the message?"

At that point, if the young man says, "Yes, yes, the message is… is… uhhhmm… sorry, I forgot," we would all look at each other rather perplexedly, wondering why did he call himself a messenger if he actually has no message?

Messengers are like the old-time mailmen who delivered letters. Mailmen don't compose those messages. They only carry those messages from one person to another person.

If we call ourselves His messengers, then we should not compose messages by way of our creative thoughts on how to present something that sounds like entertaining oratory. Rather, we must spend time in His presence in His Word, with the help of His Spirit to guide us into all truth so that after we receive His message, we simply come before His people for whom that message should be delivered and pass it along to them.

Then their reaction will be better than emotional entertainment. It will be real food for thought. Then God's people come into more of God's thoughts in both doctrinal truths and in practical and wise counsel for how our lives are to be conducted while we are upon this earth.

I wish I could tell you that God's servants who have responsibility to be in pulpits regularly really understood this, but alas, they don't. Sigh. So, I would say that much of Christendom has a love–hate relationship (or, if that's too strong, a like–dislike relationship) with the two parts of most services. The worship time is appreciated, but what follows from pulpits is rather pitiful by comparison.

- - - -

Oklahoma brother: "Yes. It's sad that soooo many Christians long for true spiritual food and are given counterfeit or junk food. Thankful that's not an issue for us."

- - - -

I recall when I visited an elderly pastor quite some years ago. I was his houseguest for Saturday night so that after breakfast at his table on Sunday morning, he would bring me to serve his flock for the first time.

When I came into his living room, the TV was on, and the pastor was listening to a rather famous personality who was holding forth in his pulpit faraway in another state. (If I named the man on TV, many would recognize that fellow, but he is deceased now.)

My host said at one point, "I like this guy. He is a very good speaker. But I have never heard him actually preach the Gospel."

The fellow on the TV was just a name to me since I had never really listened to him nor read any of his stuff. I just knew he had a big flock inside a crystal cathedral with a large following on the airwaves. So the old pastor's comment kind of surprised me. "What do you mean?" I asked.

He said, "I have never heard him tell his listeners that they were in sin and needed to repent. He never tells them that they need Jesus as Lord in their lives. His messages are all full of rhyming schemes and flowery oratory which are delightful to listen to, but where is the genuine scriptural message that people really need?"

You know, in the American context of Christendom, whenever a door is opened for me to bring the message, I am usually told before the service begins about a specific time limit that I may speak and about a schedule by which the attendees must be walking out of the sanctuary to head for lunch. Yes, I dutifully listen and then try to adhere to such guidelines. But honestly, while imparting what He has given me for them, I don't always check my watch or the clock on the wall to make sure I don't go overtime.

Then it hits me at some point to look at the time, and often I then say, "Hoo boy, I am in trouble." So I try to wind it up soon after that.

But as folks go past me at the door after the service concluded, I usually hear two kinds of comments: One of them is "I could listen to you all day," meaning they weren't angry that I seemed to overshoot my allotted time. And the other comment, expressed with a tone of incredulity, is "Pas. Douglas, today *I learned something*."

You might think that I would be thrilled by such statements, but inwardly I wince. Why? Because so many in Christendom have come to the conclusion that when it comes to whatever issues from pulpits, it is usually *not* a message from on high, and therefore they just endure all the blah blah blah as long as it doesn't make them late for their favorite eatery for lunch. Learn something? Why should they learn anything *if His servants are not equipped with real messages that need to be taught and explained?*

Do you know how I cope when I discern no real message coming forth as I sit before a pulpit? I just quietly open my Bible and tune out the blah blah blah and spend that time in His Word.

But I can testify as to how some saints overseas cope with what they regard as that unimportant segment of the service where someone is in the pulpit. A few years ago, on short notice, an invitation came from a pastor in Sumatra when he learned I was in the area. So, I agreed to come to his flock on that evening.

After the singing and worship time was done, it was time for the message. By all appearances, the pastor and his flock very much enjoyed the message and seemed to be eager listeners. Well, at least that was the case for those in that hall.

But when I concluded with a closing prayer and then I tried to hand over the mic to their pastor, he looked confused, and as he looked all around, I realized that their pattern was to have a closing song before dismissing.

But where was the song leader? Since she didn't pop up onto the stage after my prayer ended, they began calling out for her. Suddenly, from the front yard area, she heard her name, and she came trotting back inside. The moment after she took the mic from me and I sat down, what did she say next? "Oh, wasn't that a wonderful message from the American who served here tonight!"

Later, when light refreshments were served to me and a dozen others who gathered at the pastor's home, I told him to his face that we saw a clear example of hypocrisy just before the service concluded. Why should the song leader make any statement about the message when it was finally noticed that after she led the earlier songs, she exited the building to laugh and talk outside the sanctuary with her friends in the worship team? To them, their part was important, but what came next was totally unimportant. So, no need to sit down and pay attention to any message, because usually what transpired was more of a mess than a message!

Today happens to be the 17th of March, known as Saint Patrick's Day. Due to secularization accomplished by our enemy, this day is only about legends of little people called leprechauns and pots of gold at the end of rainbows and drinking green beer. Sigh.

But the spiritual origins of setting this day apart were due to the faithful diligence of an English Christian named Patrick in the fourth century who, in his teen years, was kidnapped by Irish pirates and carried off to Ireland as a slave for several years. After he escaped back to England, the Lord later put upon his heart to go back to Ireland and bring the Gospel to the snake-worshiping pagans there. Much of the nation repented. Ever since then, the Irish believers refer to Patrick as their patron saint.

When Patrick opened his mouth, what do you think the Irish folks heard? A mess? Or a message? Their hearts also burned within them as they heard a messenger who had a message from on high! Oh, how we still need this today.

- - - -

The Mess or the Message? (Part 2)

Yesterday I was blessed to have an extended chat with a sister who serves in a flock where Ruth and I spent four days recently. Here is her report:

- - - -

Thank you, Pas. Douglas, for the above message. It is very deep and thought provoking. A mess or a message. Help us Lord to bring fresh messages and not forget to preach the Gospel from the Lord to the hearers of the Word. Thank you again for that reminder.

Last night and last week, I preached on Jesus Our Great High Priest, and last night's message was about "What is Jesus doing now?"

I used your sharing with us when we were having lunch with you in our place:

1. "My blood is still *red*." Yes, His blood is still powerful to save sinners today; and

2. He is ever ready to protect us from evil. I used the video that you sent to me on Beethoven and Ted (found on YouTube, from the movie *Beethoven*).

I met a brother at the bank this morning, and he told me he was so much encouraged by last night's message and the video. He was quite down the last few days, and his spirit was uplifted again.

Thank you so much for your willingness to share. They are jewels to me.

- - - -

What an encouraging report! Thank you for sending. So glad to hear of His messages coming through you to His people.

Those of us called to be His servants in the body of Christ really need to reevaluate the importance of teaching (which is to the saved) and preaching (which is to the not-yet saved). As Paul said, the Lord has chosen one and only one method for the lost to get saved, and that is by the message getting preached (1 Cor. 1:18, 21–24).

The last part of the Great Commission tells us that "teaching" is included besides the parts about going into all the world, making disciples, and baptizing them. In fact, if the task of teaching gets minimized or left out altogether, I would contend that it is impossible to actually make new believers into mature, committed disciples for Jesus.

But the kind of teaching I am talking about isn't like what most of His servants get exposed to in various Bible Schools and/or seminaries. That stuff is very academic and analytical and is considered very scholarly. We don't need more scholars, in my opinion. We need more shepherds who can actually teach and feed their flocks with the milk and meat of what's in His Word; otherwise, His flock, after getting saved, are just starving to death! Jesus warned that when He comes back, He will deal with and discipline harshly those servants who gave into laziness, who said in their hearts, "My master won't return for a long, long time" (Matt. 24:45–51).

It is high time to get back to feeding the flock of Jesus. If you are bold enough (and I think you are), go take a look at a very hot chapter. Why is it so hot? You can feel the heat of His anger coming off the pages in Ezekiel 34. And with whom is the Lord angry? Is it with a bunch of idolatrous pagans? Nope. He is angry with the shepherds of Israel, and you can tell, He isn't talking about shepherds with baa baa sheep. He means those folks who were supposed to be spiritual shepherds for the people of His flock.

And why was it that those shepherds whom the Lord will deal with would ever actually get close to their flocks? Only because they wanted to *get something from them*!

You and I must watch over our hearts as to *why* we are approaching His flock. Are we just seeking for the praises of men? Are we trying to be comedians in the pulpit? Are we eagerly looking for large cash honorariums if they are pleased with our messages? *Or* are we approaching them because we want to take heed to our ministries to fulfill them (as Archippus was exhorted by Paul to do [Col. 4:17]) and thus please our Lord who entrusted that task of feeding sheep to us? (John 21:15–17).

We teachers of His Word are not looking for the praises of many. No. We intend to seek the praise of one voice alone, when we can hear Him one day utter to us after we enter His glorious presence, "Well done, thou good and faithful servant!" (Matt. 25:21).

- - - -

Amen. I always direct my messages to the altar call for souls opening their hearts to receive Christ as their Savior or encourage the brothers and sisters to be bold and go to share the Gospel. We must see the urgency of the Lord coming back and souls to turn to Him.

Thank you for reminding me and cautioning me to be careful not to seek the praises of many but only from Him whom we serve.

I have three weeks break before I preach again. I am going to do an in-depth study of Ezekiel, not an easy one to understand.

- - - -

Well, you may know the riddle which asks, "How do you eat an elephant?"

And the answer is, "One bite at a time."

Ezekiel has forty-eight chapters. So, pick a certain quantity that you can handle, say three chapters a day. Then across two to three weeks, you have made a complete circuit through that book.

God gave him quite a few visions. Don't let the content of some of those more mysterious passages throw you for a loop. Just recognize this about our Lord and His Word.

When He wants to speak plainly, He does so. When He wants to be obtuse, He is very deliberate about that too.

Don't belabor the obtuse stuff. Sure, read it, and then tell Him, "Ok, when You want that passage to make sense to me, then You will get through to my mind what You mean there. Until then, I will press on into the other parts that seem much more clear in its meaning."

- - - -

I just listen to Pas. David Jeremiah messages on Ezekiel 38 and 39. And I am motivated to read this book of Ezekiel. Like when you came over, you talked about how Jesus took His blood to the original temple in Heaven, and that motivated me to read and study the book of Hebrews, and I am glad I did read and study them and now able to thank Jesus for being the High Priest.

- - - -

Yes, Hebrews is often called the fifth Gospel, as it tells us much about Jesus in His ongoing ministry post-resurrection, both what He has accomplished soon after He rose from the dead and His ongoing ministry as High Priest on our behalf.

- - - -

Amen. I am truly blessed reading Hebrews and value the salvation I have in Jesus.

- - - -

That is something that I have taught about, how so many brethren, after a number of years of being saved, often no longer highly value their salvation and what it took for the Lord to secure it for us. Peter said that if the eight qualities (II Peter 1:5-8) that should be in every believer's life are missing, it is because we have become forgetful of the *great* work He did to get us forgiven and saved (II Peter 1:9).

- - - -

I agree. 🙏 As I start to read Ezekiel, the Holy Spirit will enlighten me, just like when I read Hebrews three weeks ago.

- - - -

From a brother who helps lead worship in an Oklahoma flock, after he read “The Mess or the Message?”, he sent the following:

- - - -

I enjoyed that message. I was mesmerized by the story of the song leader. One of the things I’ve always told my pastor is that my job is to prepare the congregation for the message.

I like my music, and the songs themselves will carry a message if the people will pay attention to the words (which I’m always reminding them to do). I try to listen to God’s voice and do what He says, singing the songs I feel He wants done and relay what I’m told.

Many times what I say and the very songs themselves coincide with the message of the pastor. Then I know the spirit is alive in the church (or at least in me). Once I finish, my focus is on the speaker, to hear the message God has given. My Bible is usually open to the passage/passages being discussed, and I’m making notes on the things that are talking to me.

Thank you for the message you sent. I’m always thirsty for God’s messages. Sometimes I’m surprised where I might hear them, but I'm always trying to stay in prayer as Paul stated and keep my heart open to hear what needs to be heard.

- - - -

Thanks for all your thoughtful feedback.

I can tell you that on another occasion, while I was serving a flock of *Orang Asli* (original people; they predate the emigrations of Malays from Sumatra, Chinese from China, and the Indians from either South India or Sri Lanka to Malaysia), the worship team there were a group of young adults who vigorously led us in praise and worship.

But when I was asked to come forward to bring the message, none of the worship team were in that hall. They all exited stage right to a back room in that facility where they could laugh and chitchat while the message was being heard by the older members of that flock.

I have vowed in my heart that if or when I get another open door to come serve that group of brethren again, I will go block that door with my body. If anyone tries to get past me before I start the message, I will tell them to go find a seat and get ready to learn something from His Word.

- - - -

Thy Kingdom or My Kingdom?

While at a nearby fellowship meeting yesterday for His servants in this part of the peninsula, I felt prompted at our concluding moments to ask if I could relate a story. They graciously said yes.

There was a pastor I met in Arlington, Texas, many years ago. When he was younger and still single, he volunteered to go abroad to South Africa for a full year. His duties meant that during the one-year furlough of a missionary family who had just completed a four-year term of service, this young evangelist would help to keep the ball rolling in that part of the world while that family would be absent from their field.

The evangelist had a heart fervent to preach the Gospel. He wanted to win lost souls. Having no other family ties or concerns, he busied himself with trips to many villages and remote areas where there were no churches planted yet. He didn't care about equipment nor felt the need for buildings to rent for those crusades.

God certainly blessed his efforts. Simple meetings held under a large tree or in a farmer's field would attract local attention. Folks came who were hungry for truth. The gospel message satisfied many. Lots of newcomers entered His Kingdom in Jesus' name.

The young servant from America knew that once people come to the Lord Jesus, they need to be formed into local churches. But that particular denomination had a rule which stated that before a new church could be opened, the evangelist had to find the nearest church to that venue where the crusades were taking place. Then he must seek permission from that pastor to open a new church.

The evangelist became heartbroken. He said that not a single request to open a new church was granted. Even if the venue was ten miles away or further from the nearest existing church of that denomination, every pastor gave that evangelist the same reply, which was "No! Just send over to me all of your new converts."

Most of these folks were from poor, simple villages. They did not own cars or motorbikes. They walked everywhere they went. It was not reasonable to expect these new converts who are now babes in Christ to make such a commitment to walk ten miles to attend weekly services.

In the Lord's prayer, using Old English, we say, "Thy Kingdom come, Thy will be done on earth as it is in Heaven." But many pastors around the world don't seem to have a Kingdom mentality, unless you change the prayer from "Thy Kingdom" to "my kingdom."

There are many lovely ways for a man and woman to meet, fall in love, and then commit to each other as covenant marriage partners. Then that loving couple in the midst of the blessed marriage bed can obtain one or more children from that special gift of intimacy. That is how the vast majority of humanity is conceived. But there are a few folks in this world who get their start in a terrible and violent way, when a wicked man overpowers and abuses a woman and, as a result, she becomes pregnant.

Why is it that when you seek the origins of a certain church or even the birth of an entire denomination, it traces back to strife among brethren? Yet this is one of the seven things hated by our Lord, according to Solomon (Prov. 6:16–19). The early church would experience fresh love and intimacy with her Lord, and thereafter one church would become a mother church who went on to birth many daughter churches.

Isn't this astounding? New church planting isn't always hindered by the devil or worldly governments who try to block such. The birth of new flocks can be stymied by church leaders who follow what James calls "wisdom from below," which is described as selfishly ambitious (James 3:14, 16).

So which is it? Thy Kingdom or my kingdom?

- - - -

My Sheep or His Sheep?

One response from a nearby church planter to that last article called "Thy Kingdom or My Kingdom?" was the following:

"Ha ha! Pas. Douglas, we have gone through the same difficulty to start a new church, especially here in Penang."

So I sent back the following reply to add to this topic. Hope you too are blessed.

- - - -

Do you know what I call it when you were/are up against in your church planting efforts? I call it the businessman's mentality.

If you are the only kiosk in the entire neighborhood selling bottles of Coca-Cola, then you have a monopoly, and you the seller are very happy about that. If anyone nearby wants a coke, ya gotta go buy from that one kiosk, that single proprietor.

But let word spread in that neighborhood that someone else just opened a kiosk selling bottles of coke, does the first proprietor rejoice over this development? No! He is very angry because he sees the second guy as competition! And in fact, it is a competition when this happens in the business world.

But you and I aren't called to become businessmen, but rather servants of the Lord. So we are *not* in competition with each other.

In fact, often I tell groups of pastors this:

There's enough sinners out there to grow every church.

If a young couple who recently married comes to church one Sunday and starts to share their special news that they are expecting a child soon, then the church family watches her tummy get bigger and bigger over the next eight to nine months. Then one Sunday, that couple comes to church, and the wife's tummy is much flatter, and in her arms is a precious wrapped bundle.

What is the reaction of that church family to that sight? Oh, they rush over and squeal and say, "Lemme see, lemme see! Oh, look, she has your eyes, and his nose," and they all rejoice with this family as they welcome this little one into the world.

But what if, just what if, there was a sourpuss personality present, and he marches over to the gathered gaggle of friends and well-wishers and glares at the child and declares, "Is that what I think it is? Did you two do the unthinkable and brought into this world another mouth to feed?! I cannot believe how irresponsible some people can be in today's society!" And he continues to fuss about this newborn child.

What will someone who is brave enough do at that point? He will step in front of that whining complaining creep and tell him plainly, "You are out of line, buddy. The healthy birth of this baby is not something to complain about, but to rejoice in the Lord. So, if you're gonna be so negative, then it's time for you to take a hike and leave this place of joy… *Now!*"

Yet what I have described is what happens time and again when an obedient servant is working to start a new church. The other church leaders in the area don't rejoice over this new birth, but rather denigrate his efforts and accuse him of trying to steal their sheep.

I heard another good story once. An angry pastor marched up to another pastor and accused him of stealing his sheep. Do you know what the second pastor said? He calmly replied, "Well-fed sheep cannot be stolen."

True words, indeed!

Here's another tale from a nation of 22 million, but only 4 million are people. eighteen million are baa baa sheep in the land called New Zealand.

Two boys grew up together out in the rural areas where most folks raised sheep. When they finished high school, one decided to go to university and later became a successful businessman and lived in the big city, enjoying modern life there, while his childhood friend opted to carry on as a shepherd in the grass-covered hills in the countryside.

After many years, the city fella decided to go look up his friend in the rural setting. He found him faithfully watching over a flock.

After chatting and catching up on each other's news, the city guy had an idea. He suggested that the two of them should walk behind some trees nearby, switch clothes and hats, and then walk back out into the view of the sheep. The shepherd agreed to this little experiment.

Now the disguised businessman thought he could call out to the flock and say the same things he had witnessed the shepherd had done recently. He expected the sheep to be fooled into following him across the pasture.

To his surprise, when the sheep heard him call out to them, they all lifted their heads and just stared at him for a moment. Then they all turned around and walked away from him.

The city fella was shocked. He turned to his shepherd friend and asked, "Won't any of them follow me?" And the real shepherd smiled and replied, "Oh yes… the sick ones will follow you."

If a servant has a shepherd's heart, then the sheep will know that fact. A shepherd is concerned to feed his flock, to lead his flock, and, when necessary, to rise up and protect his flock. Frankly there are many who in their younger days when they first received God's calling to become a shepherd were very diligent in fulfilling these tasks for the flock. But as the years pass, and a degree of success comes, that same shepherd can become lazy or lax in these duties. Hungry sheep, neglected sheep, and abused sheep will not continue to follow those servants.

And Peter reminds us that one title for our Lord is that He is the **Chief Shepherd** (I Peter 5:4). What does that mean? It means every shepherd down here has a Boss, and therefore the shepherds upon the earth are all under-shepherds. Those sheep are not really your sheep. They are Jesus' sheep. And we who are called to serve His flock will have to answer to the Chief Shepherd one day.

Will there be a reward for lazy shepherds? No, there will be discipline for such, says Jesus (Matt. 24:45–51).

- - - -

Who Has Holy Blood?

A pastor friend who is pioneering a flock in recent years in a small town in Central Texas just exchanged a few texts with me about the last two articles I had sent him, titled "My Sheep or His Sheep?" and "Thy Kingdom or My Kingdom?" Hope you are blessed by the concluding story:

- - - -

How is the flock doing in your neck of the woods these days, my brother? Please give them my greeting.

- - - -

Doing good, brother. I'll let them know you checked on them.

- - - -

Very good. Hope you enjoyed those last two articles.

- - - -

Yes sir. They ministered to me on my next two messages.

- - - -

Glad to hear that. Anything I can do to bless and help His servants become richer in the things of His Word, that's what I am here for.

- - - -

Very excellent timing on those two, brother.

- - - -

Here's a short story for you along these lines:

Soon after moving to Indonesia in 1986 and still learning the language, as I would meet pastors there, I learned to ask what seemed like a simple question, which was, "*Dimana gerejamu?*" (Translation: Where is your church?)

But after a while, I sensed that the Lord wasn't real happy with how I phrased this query. So I later changed the question to, "*Dimana gereja yang saudara melayani?*" (Translation: Where is the church that you serve?)

So what's the difference? The second question removes ownership of the church from that pastor to… whom? Oh, I know, because Jesus said, "Upon this rock, I will build **My church**."

So every church belongs to the One who bled, died, and rose for her, and that would be none other than Jesus!

Now when I hear a pastor say, "*Inilah gerejaku*" (this is my church), I respond, "Really? Wow! When did you die for this church? Oh? You haven't ever died yet? Well then, you misspoke because I know the One who did die for this church to buy her with His own precious holy blood. Do you have holy blood? No? Oh, well then, even if you did die for this church, your blood could not purchase her with unholy blood."

\- - - -

Amen, brother.

\- - - -

God's House: Tabernacle or Temple?

My recent articles have prompted comments and questions concerning money matters in His churches, as well as asking how important it is for a local church to have a building.

A brother in Texas who has been a longtime active member of the Gideon's Ministry wrote me to say, "We run into this attitude all the time. Even though we are an evangelistic worldwide ministry, the pastor is fearful that we will take money out of his coffers."

A brother in the southern Caribbean wrote to ask, "What would be the necessity of a building? A big one? A luxurious one? Is it our responsibility to build a building for His church? Or does He need no building but only a good shepherd? A good shepherd leads His church to green pastures and streams of water. Are those things equal to a building?"

This topic arises from a couple of errant assumptions in Christendom everywhere. If one starts from an idea conveyed in the verse, "Bring the whole tithe into **the storehouse** so that there may be food **in My house**, and test Me now in this if I will not open for you the windows of heaven, and pour out for you a blessing until it overflows" (Mal. 3:10), then which of the five ministries (from Eph. 4:11) most closely identifies itself with a building? That would be the pastors since most have (or work to obtain) a meeting place which is called a church.

Frankly, I prefer to call it a sanctuary because the original definition of *church* is found in Matt. 18:20 when Jesus declared that if just "two or three gather together in My name, there I will be in the midst of them." At that point and throughout the thirty-five years recorded about the early churches in the book of Acts, no buildings or sanctuaries are mentioned as needful by each of those bodies of Christ.

Many times, while I teach inside a sanctuary, folks will witness me walking over to the nearest wall, patting it with my hand, and hearing me say, "I am grateful for each and every venue where the followers of our Lord Jesus can gather in His name, worship Him, and hear His messages taught. But this thing I am touching now is not the church. The church is the believers that I am gazing upon right in front of me."

So, since modern-day pastors are most closely associated with buildings (instead of with groups of gathered believers), then a second error follows from this first assumption, which is that pastors are the heavenly designated administrators who oversee *all* of the tithes and offerings that are brought into that house.

Then all other ministries who function along the lines of the other four callings, or the four kinds of servants, such as apostles (which means "sent ones," i.e., missionaries), prophets, evangelists, and teachers, must kowtow, bow, and scrape (or genuflect) before those who have the calling of pastor in order to be thrown some crumbs of support. Then those four should show exuberant gratitude and say (in old Southern lingo), "Thanky, massa, thanky thanky much, massa."

Don't get me wrong. I am all in favor of every servant of the Lord to be grateful for the supply that our Lord provides. But when pastors hold a condescending attitude toward other ministries and other callings, I wish they would go back and take another look at that single long, long sentence penned by Paul who was led by the Spirit to compose what we call six verses, those being Eph. 4:11–16.

In the Greek New Testament, even if you don't understand that lingo, they used the same punctuation that is common today, that being mostly commas and periods (or some of you call "full stops"). Open that type of New Testament, and you will see for yourself that once you begin your scan at verse 11, you will not reach a period until the end of verse 16.

Now why is that detail important? Because it means that no one has the right to tinker with nor emphasize one part of that long statement and then ignore the rest. **It must be taken as an indivisible unit.**

So here is the breakdown of those six verses:

Verse 11 lists the five kinds of ministry gifts which Jesus gives, only one of which is pastors.

Verse 12 tells us why Jesus gives these five kinds of servants to the churches, that is, for their upbuilding.

Verses 13–16 relates what will be all of the consequences and blessings that will arise for every church **if verses 11 and 12 are allowed and supported to fulfill their ministries.**

Briefly, what are those blessings? Maturity, a fullness of Christ, no longer children, not easily tricked or deceived, growing up into the Head (Jesus), growth of the body, and building itself up in love.

Do those sound good to you? Do you want to see those blessings become manifest in the flock where you are? If yes, then what must happen first? We must value equally each kind of servant, support each one prayerfully and financially, and allow each one to have its time and place to serve local churches on a regular basis.

When Malachi teaches about tithing, he expressly said why the Lord wants this to happen. That prophet said, "… so there will be food in My house." Why does God want food in His house? Not because God is hungry, but because the people He has called into various ministries still have natural bodies with natural needs to be cared for.

And who or what is it that is meant by the phrase "My house"? Peter certainly clarifies that matter. "And coming to Him (Jesus) as to a living stone, rejected by men, but choice and precious in the sight of God, **you** (plural, y'all) also, as living stones, **are being built up as a spiritual house** for a holy priesthood, to offer up spiritual sacrifices acceptable to God through Jesus Christ" (1 Pet. 2:4, 5). So the born-again people of God become the houses of God, and not their meeting places.

Am I heading for the conclusion to get rid of all church sanctuaries? No, not really. But I wish we would keep in mind what the Lord's attitude is toward the building of sanctuaries. In the Old Testament days, there were two structures associated with God's people and the worship of the Lord, those being, first, the Tabernacle, and then later, the Temple.

Now consider who initiated the origins of both of those structures. Was Moses sitting around one day soon after the Red Sea closed over the top of the Egyptian chariots, horses, and soldiers and asking himself, "What should we do next? Hmm… Oh I know. Let's make a Tabernacle for the Lord!"

No. We have seven chapters of detailed instructions that Moses received **from the Lord** about making the Tabernacle and all of its furnishings (Exod. 25–31).

Now compare that with the origins of the first Temple. Whose idea was that? David is now king and secure upon his throne. And one day, he thinks to compare himself with the Ark of the Covenant. Where does David dwell? In a lovely expensive palace. But where is the Ark of God? It dwells in a simple tent. Yet the Ark represents the living presence of the Lord in the midst of His people forever, while David will only be on the earth for a short span of time.

So David speaks out loud in his court his newly formed idea to build a big beautiful sanctuary for the Lord. Nathan the prophet hears what David proposes, and his first response is, "Go, do all that is in your mind, for the Lord is with you" (II Sam. 7:3).

Oops. Have you ever spoken too soon? I have no room to throw stones at Nathan. That night, that prophet got a word of correction from the Lord. Go read verses 4–7, and see for yourself that the Lord had been satisfied since His people left Egypt to dwell in a tent called the Tabernacle. The Lord had never rebuked any leader saying, "Why haven't you built for Me a house of cedar?"

So what did the Lord do? Did He forbid them to build a house for Him? No, He permitted them to build a Temple, but He never required them to build such. This proposal was man's idea, not God's idea.

And even when the first Temple was dedicated in the days of Solomon, what warning did the Lord give His people? Go read nine verses to find this answer, found at 1 Kings 9:1–9. The summary is this: "Be faithful to Me in the Covenant, and I will receive your worship in this Temple, but forsake Me by not faithfully keeping the Covenant, and then I will not just abandon this structure. I will flatten it."

Do you think the Lord meant what He said? Twice they have built for Him a Temple. Twice it has been torn down with not one stone left upon another, as Jesus predicted (Matt. 24:1, 2). Yet both Temples were lovingly built and had great beauty.

Are you familiar with the expression to "worship the Lord in the beauty of holiness"? Yet we can do as the Old Covenant people did and allow this to become reversed so that we think that we can worship Him in the holiness of beauty. That is why even today, many sanctuaries are lavishly decorated and no expense is spared to adorn that great hall for our worship services.

So yes, the Lord allowed them to build for Him a Temple, and in like manner, He will allow us to build for Him a sanctuary. But if we do not continue to walk with Him in holiness in the New Covenant, then He will again abandon those meeting places. They will become just monuments to an earlier time when we did walk with our Lord in holiness and obeyed Him.

You can go through huge cathedrals in Europe and elsewhere as a tourist to admire the architecture and the artwork therein, but there are no more meetings inside of two or three who gather in His name, so therefore there is no more manifest presence of the Lord Jesus in those places.

If we would take a page out of the early church playbook, they cared little about structures. Anyone's home or courtyard, or down by the river under a large shade tree, was a sufficient place to meet for services. Their priority was to know the living Lord Jesus being manifested through His various servants (not just pastors) that He had called who would seek to fulfill those ministries which would result in their growth and maturity. If we would be satisfied with simple venues in which to meet, then we could channel more of the tithes and offerings for the proper support of all His servants who still have stomachs so that there would be sufficient food in His house.

- - - -

Who Is the Big C?

A fellow servant in this land and I have exchanged several texts since we first met about six weeks ago. She will soon be in front of the flock to bring another message. After relating a synopsis of what the Lord has given her so far, she asked for my advice on what else to keep in mind concerning the topic of perseverance. The following is what I just composed and sent her. I hope you too are blessed:

- - - -

There are three words that are synonymous terms in our New Testament, which are endurance, steadfastness, and perseverance. The only thing I would caution you about when lifting these things up before the saints is this: any exhortation to them to keep trying, keep believing, and keep on obeying sounds like an appeal to our willpower.

But it is not my willpower that is more precious than gold to my Lord but rather my faith in Him even while under duress (i.e., while facing persecution, etc.) that is more precious than gold to our Lord, according to 1 Pet. 1:6, 7.

When we look for an illustration of this dynamic, go back and check again the story of Peter's promised faithfulness to Jesus, even unto death, beginning with John 13:36–38. Why does Peter make such a strong declaration to follow Jesus even to death? Because Peter believes in the strength of his own will to make and keep such a commitment.

But what does he hear Jesus reply to this proposition? Peter hears a prediction from Jesus that in just a few short hours, Peter will utterly fail to keep his promise of faithfulness and instead will do the unthinkable, which is to even deny knowing who Jesus is before a rooster awakens to cock-a-doodle-do!

At that point, I would contend that many Bible readers would say, "Oh look, I have reached the end of a chapter, so it is time to stop reading in John until tomorrow, and I will begin then with chapter 14." But there is no good reason to stop reading because the time and setting and particularly the interaction that is transpiring between Jesus and Peter are uninterrupted!

So if you were Peter and you had just heard this horrible prediction from Jesus and you still believed in the power of your own will to stay faithful to Jesus no matter what (including the threat of death), what did Peter do? Whether he gestured physically by shaking his head back and forth to indicate "No! I don't believe that will happen" or he just silently in his heart rejected that statement, Jesus knew what was going on inside of Peter. And now John 14:1 makes great sense as to why Jesus made that next declaration to Peter in particular, which was, "Let not your heart be troubled; believe in God, believe also in Me."

Surely any prediction of Peter's faithfulness proving itself a failure would indeed be very troubling to Peter. But that failure does not and will not shock or surprise Jesus because He already knows about mankind's flawed and corrupted willpower. Jesus directs Peter to quit having faith in himself and in the power of his own will and instead to put his faith in the Father and in Jesus Himself. That is the context of why John 14:1 says what it says and why it is imparted at that very moment and that it is primarily directed straight to Peter, even though everyone in the room heard this entire interaction between Peter and Jesus.

And of course, when Peter's failure became manifest, and for the third time he denied knowing Jesus, then the rooster crowed, what was Peter's reaction? Peter went off to a place alone to cry bitterly. What was he crying about? He had discovered the hard way that his own willpower had indeed failed him.

So when I read passages like Rev. 1:9 and II Thess. 3:5, what am I directed to notice that is found in our Jesus? While alone on Patmos island, John said that he was a fellow partaker in three things with all the other saints, those being the things of tribulation and kingdom **and perseverance** which are in

Jesus. Paul said to the churches in Thessalonica, "May the Lord direct your hearts into the love of God, **and into the steadfastness of Christ Jesus**" (II Thess. 3:5).

There was a movement in Christendom in the United States quite a few years ago called Promise Keepers. It was oriented toward the brothers in Christ Jesus. They held large rallies in stadiums or other venues where thousands of men could gather to hear famous men give stirring messages to inspire men to make renewed commitments to be keepers of their word and their promises.

I won't say that nothing good came of these meetings. Positive testimonies arose from many men about the encouragement that they felt came to them. The fellowship of men bonding with other men was very sweet indeed.

But my main concern over that movement was there was far too much emphasis upon men and their abilities to make and keep promises without reference to the need of reliance upon the Lord Jesus to truly make possible the keeping of wedding vows and such. Yes, everyone, male and female, has a God-given will. But Scripture teaches that my sin thoroughly corrupts all of me, spirit, soul, and body. So even my willpower is corrupted, doomed to failure sooner or later if left to myself alone.

This is why I personally shy away from giving exhortations from any pulpit to say, "**you can do it**," no matter what the particular "it" is in that day's message. Instead, I want to keep pointing myself and all my hearers to the living Jesus who can do all things through me if I will just keep relying upon Him, keep calling out to Him, keep in step with Him, and keep listening to Him. Jesus. Jesus. Jesus. Not me, me, me trying.

Frankly, in recent years, I have proposed that any churchgoer bring a piece of paper or a notebook and a pen to the next service and then make three headings at the top of three columns. At the first heading, write *God*; at the second one, *you*; and at the third one, Jesus. Now you are ready to do a study.

During every song that is sung, every prayer that gets prayed, every testimony that is proclaimed, and every message that is taught, when you hear any reference to the Almighty, put a stroke under that column 'til you have put four strokes. Then at the fifth mention, put a cross stroke over those first four straight strokes. Do likewise for every mention about you, the listener, you, the saint, and what you are exhorted to do. Then compile a set of strokes in the third column every time you hear the name of Jesus.

It is concerning to my heart that even in doctrinally sound flocks, your survey will reveal how much emphasis or mention is about God (in a very generic way) or about you and me. But the Name above all names seems to get short shrift.

What is wrong with this picture? As Paul said to the saints in Corinth, "I am afraid, lest as the serpent deceived Eve by his craftiness, your minds should be led astray from the simplicity and purity of devotion to Christ Jesus" (II Cor. 11:3).

I hope this helps you continue to prepare what are His messages directed to His people. The big C is not cancer, nor Covid, nor any crisis. The big C is Christ Jesus.

- - - -

By Faith, Not By Sight

"We walk by faith, not by sight." Those seven words were declared by Paul in a letter to the churches in Corinth, found at II Cor. 5:7. Many saints and servants can easily quote this truth even if they don't always recall it's reference.

Quite a while back, I had the opportunity to serve behind the bamboo curtain. While there, I was invited by a group of cross-cultural servants to gather with them at a home for a Sunday service. They even afforded me the opening to bring them a message, which I did.

If I were asked to tell you what were the particulars of a lesson I taught long ago, usually I must admit that I cannot remember. But in this case, I can. In that gathering in His name, I prefaced everything by saying surely the Lord would not have sent us to be His servants overseas if, firstly, we had not truly met Jesus as Lord and Savior, and, secondly, we had not already been filled with a certain amount of knowledge and truth from Him. Why send an empty-headed zero to the other side of the world? There are a lot of logistical and financial difficulties to overcome before anyone can buy tickets for their family and head off to Mambo Bambo. How is it that we would be known as messengers of the Lord of Hosts and yet have no message? Inconceivable!

And yet, I wanted to encourage my fellow workers so that our former eagerness to learn when we had been in university or seminary would not wane after we finally got through all the hoops to reach these fields abroad. It's like the answer which the Lord gave me after I realized that the proposals and promises from servants who enticed me to relocate my family to their region were sadly not fulfilled at all. In my broken-hearted state, I called out to the Lord, asking why it was that I was there at all, and His gentle reply came, "Well son, you're not out of school yet." He wasn't kidding! In those six months based in that location and ministry, He taught me things that have resonated through so much of my teaching ever since, and that all happened to me over thirty years ago.

Now I will admit that I am a slow learner, but at least I do expect to keep learning. Solomon said to "watch over your heart with all diligence, for from it are the springs of life" (Prov. 4:23). If I ever allow myself to set up camp on a certain plateau and become so comfortable there that I quit climbing higher, then the spring of truth within me will squeeze down to a trickle because when I stop learning, then I also stop teaching anything which is fresh from above.

Now that I have had decades of life and service for our Lord in many overseas contexts, I am grateful that my Heavenly Rabbi has never retired. In His earthly ministry, Jesus was called Teacher more than any other title. As He has drawn me since childhood to become a man of His Book, He has opened my eyes to notice things while in fields abroad that I never perceived as terribly important during my life before first moving overseas in 1986.

Growing up in the American context of Christendom, how much exposure does one have concerning idols? Answer: next to nothing. Oh yes, being raised in Sunday school and church and becoming a Bible reader from a young age, sure, I knew the word *idol* and that God didn't like idols. I probably had to get my dad to explain to me about the second of the Ten Commandments as to what in the world was a "graven image." Probably I was rather typical of the mindset you would encounter when meeting a WASP, a white Anglo-Saxon protestant.

But if Jesus calls such folks into world missions, I dearly hope they stay in His Word and keep learning while humbly in His presence because Western-style Christendom is weak and lacking when it comes to this topic about idols. Indeed, how can protestant schools of training take idols very seriously when it seems there are none around?

What does His Word clarify about idols and their origins? Who is it that inspires and instructs the hearts of pagans to chisel or sculpt such elaborate and expensive objects that appear to be alive with exotic powers?

Throughout the Old Testament, you notice something called *testimonies*. The writer reminisces about the stories that were generated in a former time. Psalm 106 is an example of such. It is forty-eight verses in length, but from verse 6 through 46, one testimony after another is related, hailing back to the era of Moses and going forward to the period of the Judges.

One particular paragraph is very revealing. Read the six verses from 34 to 39. Verse 36 refers to idols, verse 37 to demons, and verse 38 again comes back to the term idols.

Before Moses died, he had already instructed the Hebrews what God's people were to do about those pagan people and about their objects of worship as soon as they would follow Joshua into the Promised Land. The various nations ensconced there were called the Amorites. Way back as far as the days of Abraham, God had promised to give Abraham's descendants all of that land someday, but not just yet. Why not? Because "the iniquity of the Amorite is not yet complete" (Gen. 15:16).

God Almighty is patient, and Paul explained that His reason for being so long suffering is because He gives mankind multiple opportunities to repent (Rom. 2:4). Peter says likewise in II Peter 3:9. Our Lord takes no delight in the death of the wicked (Ezek. 18:23, 32).

Yet across that next period of 400 years, the Amoritic people chose not to repent. They clung to their idols, and the demons behind those idols inspired those folks to commit flagrant acts of immorality and even child sacrifice (Psalm 106:28–31, 37, 38).

Have you ever heard of the nakedness chapter in the Bible? It is nestled into the midst of the least read book of the entire Bible, that being Leviticus. Read chapter 18 about God's guidelines on who should see someone's naked condition and who should not. Then notice what He reveals about the Amoritic people who already inhabit the Promised Land. The Lord says that those idol-worshiping pagans have been ardent practitioners in violating God's holy standards in these matters, and therefore they have forfeited their rights to continue dwelling in that land. God says their land has become defiled by all of their lewdness and immorality, and thus it is the land itself that will spew them out when Joshua and the Hebrews come marching in (Lev. 18:24–30).

Flip over to Deut. 18:9–14. God revealed that the Amorites were also heavily into witchcraft, the occult, and talking to the dead. This is why the Lord was going to drive them out before Joshua and His people.

In Deut. 9:4–6, the Lord repeats something three times. It is *not* because His people are so righteous that He is giving them the victories which will result in taking over the Promised

Land. It is only because of the "wickedness of these nations that the Lord is dispossessing them before you."

Frankly, as a youth, the simplistic overview I had of the Old Testament stories of Joshua conquering those people was such that I actually faulted the Lord as being terribly harsh. I thought, "How terrible for all those nice innocent people who already lived there to be condemned and killed because God was helping Joshua to do that!"

Now I know better. God had patiently reached out to them all for hundreds of years to bring about repentance, but they resisted and rejected all of His overtures. Instead they clung to their idols, and the demons behind those idols led them into extremely serious wickedness. They were not nice innocent people. Those who adhere to idols walk by sight, not by faith in the unseen Almighty God.

If modern-day saints from the West could be transported back to the age of the early church in the first century, then those passages in our New Testament about Paul's teaching concerning idols would make more sense to us. Look up 1 Cor. 10:14–22, which starts with, "Flee from idolatry." I never saw a single idol during my childhood, so what was I supposed to run away from?

But Paul also makes this same connection between idols and demons (1 Cor. 10:19–21), which no one ever taught me about while I dwelt in the West, even during my preparation for overseas missions.

So guess what I had to learn the hard way? Through a very painful experience which took years to recover from, I found out that the Lord was as serious as a heart attack when it comes to His divine instructions in regard to idols. As the cup bearer said to the pharaoh, "I would make mention today of my own sins" (Gen. 41:9).

Long ago, when my family had only nineteen months experience in Southeast Asia during my first term overseas, we were on a trip into two areas of Thailand. A non-Christian contact in Bangkok was a high-ranking official in the government. He treated us to a very nice meal and also offered to bring us on a personal tour of the Palace Grounds. This man actually had a parking slot reserved just for his BMW on those grounds.

While walking from building to building, seeing all of the unique architecture and artwork on various walls, he asked us if we wanted to step inside and see the Emerald Buddha (which actually is green jade). Knowing what I do now, I should have politely turned him down, and we should have walked elsewhere.

But in my ignorance of God's Word on this matter, we just smiled and followed him into that Temple. No one was allowed to just walk inside. Everyone who would enter must first take off one's shoes just outside the big double doors as a sign of respect for that idol. So we all took off our shoes before we entered.

Indeed the official who brought us there not only took off his shoes but also, just after entering, kneeled down and bowed to the floor with hands clasped together in an act of prayerful worship for a few seconds. We just stared upward toward that green idol on the far side of the building, and then we all went outside and reclaimed our footwear.

There I was, a servant of the Lord Jesus, sent into His fields abroad, yet entering a realm designated for the worship of our Lord's enemy and showing that demon respect by taking off my shoes and gazing upon an image inspired by that demon! What is wrong with this picture? As Paul admonished his readers, "You cannot drink the cup of the Lord and the cup of demons; you cannot partake of the table of the Lord, and the table of demons" (1 Cor. 9:21).

This is why the Lord directed the Hebrews that they had to do more than conquer the Amoritic people. Their idols and objects of worship had to be destroyed and removed from the land also (Deut. 7:24–26). Why? Because those things are like welcome mats to the demons behind them!

A man may own a yacht who lives in Key West, Florida. One sunny day, the sea is calm, and there's a fine breeze blowing. So this man decides to go sailing but not paying attention closely to his navigation; after several hours heading south, what does he see on the horizon? There's some land, so he steers that way to go explore, thinking he will have a nice picnic on a sandy beach under a coconut tree.

But lo and behold, just before he reaches the shore, a power-boat pulls up with armed men in uniform who don't look too friendly, and he sees rifles aimed at him. He is ordered to drop sail and anchor. He asks, "What's the problem?" Turns out he sailed right into Cuban waters, and he is under arrest, and his boat will be confiscated by the Cuban government! But he protests, saying that he didn't know where he was. Will his ignorance be an adequate defense so that he won't go to a Cuban prison for a long time? No, it will not. Have you ever heard the saying, "Ignorance of the law is no excuse"?

So what happened to Douglas after ignorantly walking into that Temple? Do you recall Jesus telling Peter that Satan had demanded of Heaven to sift Peter like wheat? (Luke 22:31) Methinks my enemy made the same demand of me. I stepped into his territory. I showed respect for his object. Quite possibly, a holy angel also followed me into that place since they render aid to those who will inherit salvation (Heb. 1:14), thus further infuriating those unholy spirits.

Four days after that Thai trip finished, it was time to leave my family for a ten-day trip to Singapore to help a brother who was pioneering a new flock there. Unbeknownst to me, ol' Slewfoot was waiting for me on a wet sidewalk that sloped downward. While trying to run in the rain from the taxi to the KFC soon after I landed, both of my feet shot out from under me. My body flipped over so quickly that my last view before impacting the concrete below me was seeing both feet up against the sky. It was my upper back that smacked that unforgiving surface.

Then the screaming began. That was me. I couldn't help myself. The shooting pain was indescribable. People rushed to help me. Someone called an ambulance. I was taken to a nearby hospital. Two sets of X-rays and three doctors agreed that I had suffered a compression fracture of the T3 vertebrae (that's between my shoulder blades) plus a cracked rib. I stayed one night and left with a bunch of pain killers (which didn't live up to that term) and muscle relaxers since modern medicine still doesn't know how to stretch a squished bone back to its original size.

About two weeks later, I was advised to quit those meds since they were considered habit forming. I did so but then soon regretted following that counsel. For a full year thereafter, I could not lay horizontally in bed longer than four hours. Though still tired, I would awaken with shooting pain in my back. Had to get up, fill an old-fashioned hot water bottle with boiling water, flip it onto the middle of my back, and then sit in a chair for an hour waiting for the pain to die down. Then I went back to bed for another four hours and repeated what I had done in the wee hours to get some relief again. No therapy, meds, or treatments of any kind in either Asia or in America could really help me.

May I ask you, does your flock support someone who serves cross-culturally somewhere in the world? It isn't uncommon for American churches who do so to have a wall or a display case of mission-related artifacts which have been graciously given to those brethren by a missionary whom they help as a token of that servant's gratitude. Although well intentioned, I must caution you that certain objects ought *not* to be bought, kept, carried, or displayed anywhere by any believers whatsoever. Those items are not just curious-looking oddities from faraway lands. They are not just things that reflect a different kind of culture—they are directly associated with demons and demonic activities.

Let me testify how the Lord prevented me from making this kind of mistake. Before starting a furlough, I too am mindful to go shopping for artifacts and things that will be part of my table displays as I present mission programs to our support base of churches.

Have you ever seen a kind of knife where the blade looks like a wriggling snake from the hilt to the point? Over here, it's called a kris, pronounced creese. They are very common to find anywhere souvenirs are sold. They're seen on the local currency. Multiple sizes are available from very small to the full-size ones like the king wears on his ceremonial belt.

So before a furlough began, I figured I should go shopping to get a kris knife. But I would get this strange feeling inside, sort of like nausea. Finally I asked the Lord, "Is there something wrong with my trying to buy a kris?" He prompted me to go find some local believers and ask them about the kris.

When I did, they got wide-eyed, like maybe it was a taboo subject. Here's what I learned. When a man over here hates someone and wants to do him harm but without getting arrested for actual violence against his enemy, what can he do? He gets a kris and then goes through a ceremony, seeking the help of a spirit. Then he watches for his enemy to walk by so that the fresh footprint of that man is easily seen in the ground. He brings the empowered kris with him and then stabs the kris into that footprint. At that moment, his enemy will suddenly "feel" a stabbing pain in his body. Sometimes the victim will actually die from this kind of spiritual attack.

Once I knew this background to the kris knife, I realized why the Lord was getting my attention to head me away from buying a kris to bring to America and put it upon my artifacts table. Worse still, I could have bought a bunch of small ones to give away to many supporters!

Our Lord has ordained for His people to walk with Him by faith in His Word. But the realm of our enemy does the opposite. Satan inspires sinners to make idols and objects which are seen by natural eyes. Thus they walk by sight, not by faith.

And Hosea has a word for those brethren who dwell in lands where few if any idols are present to be seen. In the middle of Hosea 14:3, that prophet says, "… we will not say again 'Our god' to the work of our hands." Have you ever heard it said, "Oh, he idolizes his car" or maybe "she idolizes her beauty"? Whatever can be seen with natural eyes can become an idol.

Let us love and trust in the unseen Lord of Heaven and not allow our hearts to love the things of this world. Then the Lord will be close to His people, and the enemy kept at bay.

\- - - -

By Faith, Not By Sight (Part 2)

After several responses to the last article, I added more stories to this discussion. Hope you are blessed, edified, and sufficiently warned.

- - - -

Very very good, my brother. Making me take a closer look at the “idols” and the demons behind them, in my life.

- - - -

So I added this:

Glad you plowed your way through that epistle. The Lord had been prompting my attention across recent weeks, especially thru those passages found in Psalm 106 and 11 Cor. 10. And I had to make it a matter of prayer over a week’s time about how to compose what I began to realize would become an unusually long article. When I composed it last night, I started writing it around 7 pm and didn't finish it 'til after 1 am.

- - - -

Obviously, Holy Spirit led my brother. GBU.

- - - -

Hold on… got a P.S. to add…

A new friend we just made while serving in Alor Setar for four days has prompted a couple more items to share as we chatted back and forth today. I will grab a copy and add them here for you also to be blessed by.

To give you another tidbit about the progress the Lord had to bring about in my life concerning this matter of idols, consider this short story.

I believe it was 1989 when the following happened between me and another missionary who had just recently relocated his home base from Bangladesh to Penang. So I already had three years of experience in this region, but he had already been in Asia more than seven years when we met.

He too, like me, is from the United States. But he already had awakened to the deadly nature and wickedness of the realm of idols before that realization had hit me.

As we chatted one day, I made mention of a certain landmark here in Penang and called it a "cute temple." Why did I think that? Well, typical of most Chinese temples, it was very brightly painted in a variety of colors so that structure had eye appeal.

But my friend gave me a wry smile and said that even though he had seen many temples in Asia, he had yet to see one that he would call cute. He already understood that those temples dedicated to Buddhism, Taoism, or Hinduism were full of idols that misled and deceived many people into wrongly giving their praise and worship unto those fallen angels who had inspired the making of all those idols.

When that friend would be in the car with me and we drove past any particular temple, he would quit talking to me for a moment and instead declared sternly, "Devil, you're a liar!" The Lord made good use of that friend in my life to help me awaken to those spiritual realities.

In our stateside travels, we are often hosted at the homes of brethren who attend the churches that make up our support base. For folks who have a much more stable lifestyle than someone like me who has frequent travels, their homes show forth a lot of attention given to their decor. Many lovely items grace their walls or fill their bookshelves or various flat places with artwork.

Some of these saints have also had various travels. So they keep a sharp eye out for new items they might acquire which become mementos of those trips.

But while I stay there, it still amazes me that next to a Cross hung on a wall can also be found a statue of a Buddha which has its place on a nearby shelf! One nice couple who had lived abroad while the husband was an exec for an oil company had a large collection of kris knives neatly displayed in one room.

Christians everywhere need to awaken to the dangers they are bringing upon their own homes by not exercising any discernment when it comes to home decoration. Those objects are welcome mats for the demons who inspired the making of those things.

Would anyone just smile at the sight when you open your front door to enter your house and you see that a muddy hungry pig is rooting around in your rubbish bin and your pantry spreading garbage and filth everywhere the pig goes? No! You would get angry, and you would chase that offending creature out of your property and then firmly shut and lock the door.

Yet what are we doing when we naively bring "pretty things" into our dwellings but, in our ignorance, we have just rung the dinner bell to the nasty demons who are associated with those objects? Who in their right mind as a Christian would like to be in close fellowship with demons in the place you call home?

As Hosea said, God's people are destroyed for lack of knowledge (Hosea 4:6).

- - - -

Got one more exchange to lay on you which you'll probably enjoy which is along these same lines.

Hold on…

- - - -

After a brother in Ft. Worth read the article called "Walk By Faith, Not By Sight," he wrote back to update me on his testimony in this subject.

- - - -

Many American Christians don't even believe the devil is real, much less that demons are real. About twenty years ago, we went to a conference on healing. I did not get much out of the conference information because I was sure the verses they were quoting were not in the Bible.

So I was looking up and reading verses before and after, and to my surprise, they are there and mean what they were saying. I had to go back about six months later to really understand what they were teaching about healing, about fear being a spirit, about the sins of Job which opened him up to be sifted by the devil, and so on.

When I talked to my pastor about what I had learned, he told me I needed to find another church.

- - - -

I added the following to this discussion like this:

Yes, your journey and mine certainly have some similarities, both of us being raised in the context of being church-goers within American Christendom. Frankly, His Word is so rich with knowledge and revelation about so many things that I see one reason behind why there are so many types and kinds of denominations popping up across the fruited plains of the United States is that each group decides they have the liberty to pick and choose which verses and topics they will hold to and emphasize while ignoring or relegating to the status of being unimportant all of the other passages.

So when you went digging through the Scriptures and discovered and studied those additional truths which your brand of church had been neglecting, you were both shocked and blessed.

This is why I tell fellow Western missionaries that I hope after they arrive to their respective fields abroad, they are still ready and open to learn more things from the local third world pastors they will encounter and labor among because those guys may not have more than a sixth grade primary school education in their background, but they have PHDs in matters like spiritual warfare, whereas the typical Western saint is still in nursery school in those things.

This is the failure we have due to our choice of adjective that we grow up with. What word is it that precedes the word Christian? There are so many descriptive words to choose from, such as saying, "I am a ____ Christian," with the blank being filled in by any denominational name, or terms such as liberal, conservative, progressive, Calvinistic, Armenian, sacramental, evangelical, charismatic, Pentecostal, holiness, Sabbatarian, and the list goes on from there.

In my opinion at this stage of my life, having been allowed by His mercy to reach the age of 66, I now only prefer one kind of adjective. I want to be and become a biblical Christian, one who continually stays in the length and breadth of the entire Book, searching it out on a daily basis while in His presence and having a heart of humility and expectation that He will continue to teach me things and will reveal more things to me, not just things about Himself or things about the future but also things that include words of additional correction of wrong ideas within my thoughts or wrong actions within my life. I think that's where He has brought you to also.

- - - -

He replied with, "Amen," and then added the following:

I agree and have seen that many many Christians don't recognize the spiritual warfare that is all too real. I believe that while we don't want to give the enemy too much credit, understanding that he is real and is constantly attacking is godly wisdom.

- - - -

Yep. And we fool around with stuff like a child trying to figure out what this green, egg-shaped thing is with a pull ring on one end, and… oh look, this pin can be pulled out, and… why is it ticking now?

How any of us survive is testament to the great mercy of our Lord who holds back the full consequences that we so richly deserve from our naive ignorance of truly deadly matters. Hand grenade anyone?

- - - -

Chicken Little?
Not For Me

A brother in Oklahoma forwarded to me a forty-seven-minute video which troubled him and wanted my feedback about what has been freshly revealed about the origins and purposes behind the worldwide pandemic. Here's how I fielded that one, and I hope you too are blessed by our back and forth chat on this topic.

- - - -

Ok, I just took in that forty-seven minute video interview in one sitting. Yes, as you said, it is eye opening.

I may generate another article soon dealing with this matter. But for now, just keep in mind a couple of basic truths. Firstly, no matter how many specific names of evil individuals and/or evil groups/agencies/government departments that can indeed be exposed with the light of truth for deliberately dealing out death on a global scale, who is it that is really behind it all? Our real enemy is the same one who rose up against his Maker and persuaded a third of the angelic realm to follow him to try to raise his throne to be equal with God Almighty and then having been cast out of Heaven like a bolt of lightning; that enemy also became the enemy of God's highest creation, mankind, who is made in His image and likeness. So the Lord God's enemy is our enemy, too, and has been ever since Adam and Eve lived in Paradise.

Secondly, the Lord revealed to Moses something very basic and easy to understand without the need for any fancy application of principles to interpret what it is that the Lord means, and that is found at Deut. 30:15–19. The Lord says that He has put before all of mankind two and only two choices. (Obviously if you have 3, 5, 10, or a 100 choices in front of you to choose from, your chances of making a wrong choice, a hurtful choice, go way up. But the Lord made things real simple for us so that even the non-geniuses like yours truly could get it.)

And what are those two choices? *Life* or *death*, the blessing or the curse.

And the Lord helps everyone who looks at this single test question, and instead of leaving it up to chance that we might make the wrong choice, the Lord helps us by telling us which one is the correct choice. "Psst… **choose life, life is the right answer**."

So the Lord Himself is life, and He creates life, and He makes possible that all organisms can also reproduce living organisms according to their kinds. Further He tells us in the fifth commandment to "honor your father and mother, that your days may be long in the land of the living." In other words, God who is life used your father and mother to create your life, and those children are to show honor to them as a way of showing the Lord that you are glad to be alive.

But our enemy already made his choice to rebel against the Living One, the source of all other living beings and creatures. So he has chosen death. And his influence ever since being cast down to the earth has never changed from trying to get mankind to agree with him to choose death.

That's also why mankind was given the sixth commandment which says, "Do not murder." Anyone who decides not to wait on the Lord's decision about how long someone should live but instead takes that matter into his own hands is proving that he has made the wrong choice, for we are told to choose life. When we choose death for one or for millions, we are choosing the curse, not the blessing, and we are bringing curses upon ourselves.

So all of these exposés, however well substantiated with truth and facts from reliable and honest sources, Christian or otherwise, should really not contain much to actually surprise the person who knows the Scriptures. We not only have a living and active Lord Jesus, but we also have an enemy who is still on the loose and sometimes referred to as the prince of the power of the air (Eph. 2:2).

How do you fight an enemy like that? Can you shoot the devil with an AR-15? No? What about giving him a swift karate chop? Can you land a physical blow upon a spirit who has neither flesh nor blood?

When the Lord clues you in that at that moment, you are face-to-face with a demonic entity, we are told what is our very effective weapon to use against him—that is the knowledge of Jesus' blood upon the mercy seat in Heaven where He Himself placed it about 2,000 years ago (Rev. 12:11). When you are face-to-face with any unsaved human and you hear all of the lies and confusion which comes out of that mouth, your weapon is truth to combat each lie. So the better you know the Scriptures, the better armed you shall be to fight back against all the lies which our real enemy has thus far deceived that person into believing are the truth.

- - - -

He replied:

I recognize that if true, there is only one source of such evil. The realization is that the end is much closer than I thought. And I thought it was close. Doesn't change anything as we simply need to keep our eyes on Jesus.

- - - -

So I added the following:

Have you ever enjoyed a live drama production, such as a Shakespeare comedy play? I recall seeing "A Comedy of Errors" back in my college days at the Ft. Worth Scott Theatre. It was an absolute hoot!

Now how long does a play run usually? Anywhere from an hour-long production by kids in high school to two hours for the professional stuff.

But have you ever been involved with producing a play? Oh my! How much time does it take to get that play ready for the public? Think about all the work put into making the props. How much money and energy went into those costumes? Then how much practice time went into rehearsals ironing out the wrinkles until all flows smoothly from scene to scene? What about music and special effects?

Short answer? You cannot put on a quality play without months of work ahead of time.

Now this has its parallels with what will play out on the world stage for all of those cataclysmic end-time events predicted in the Scriptures. The devil is working hard behind the scenes to get everything ready for his planned one world religion, one world cashless economy, one world government, and, his cherry on top, his own incarnate masterpiece, the appearance and rule of his antichrist. Once the big curtain opens, these things will be manifest and easily seen by all. But before then, years of labor are fashioning all of the props and costumes to get ready for those last days of this era.

And I have news for all my well-meaning brethren who seem to work so hard to bring out documentaries which shine the light of these many evil preparations. No matter what becomes exposed, **it will not stop the devil nor even slow him down**. It is all going to happen. The Lord already foresaw it and revealed it to a number of folks who have spoken prophetically that these things will happen.

But God's people have hopefully read the end of The Book. He wins, so we His people win also. And the devil and all who follow him will lose.

So let's take a page out of the reformer Martin Luther's playbook. After Martin discovered the truth by studying Scripture that salvation is by faith in Jesus alone, he then actually met Jesus as Lord and Savior.

One night, Martin awoke because he heard a noise somewhere in the house. He got up, left the bedroom, went down the hall, and then opened the door to his study where he had already composed many books and tracts.

And who did Martin see sitting at his desk? He saw a manifestation of the devil himself glaring at Martin. What happened next? Martin said, "Oh, it's only you," and he closed the door and went back to bed.

Let's not get too excited over all the wicked things our enemy is doing. As Jesus corrected His own disciples, "Rejoice not that the demons are subject to you, but rejoice that your names are recorded in Heaven" (Luke 10:20). We are going to enjoy Jesus forever in Heaven. And the wicked things done by our enemy will become a faint memory.

Well, I guess my answer ran a bit longer than I first thought would happen just now. Hope you are blessed and refortified in your conviction on how important His written Word is for us, especially as we come to the end of this age when deception will become more and more rampant.

- - - -

He sent back:

"Good words. Thank you, brother. Somehow comforted that you're not surprised that such evil is directly at work on such a global scale. But the depth and breadth of this deception and death in the US, frankly it surprised me."

- - - -

I concluded our chat with this:

I think I have written other articles mentioning about the Georgia Guidestones that some secretive group put up in 1980. Do you recall what guideline #1 is that is chiseled into those massive slabs of granite in several major languages?

"Keep the population of the earth to about 500,000,000."

There are now approximately 7 billion folks alive upon this planet. Do you realize what ratio those two figures are in relation to one another? They are 14 to 1.

So you and thirteen others walk into a room. One of you gets to walk out alive and carry on your life. The other thirteen need to simply go away… permanently!

Whoever came up with those guidelines think they are smarter than God Himself. God says, "Choose life." But certain folks who consider themselves the elite of this world have decided to agree with the devil to do the opposite and instead choose death for billions of people, but not for themselves, of course. Oh no, they are too important to volunteer for their own plans for human extermination on such a grand scale.

But I wish more of my brethren would calm down and ask, "Do you really believe that our God will actually allow them to succeed?" Instead, I witness so many brethren who spend too much time on the Internet and not much time in His Word daily running around, sounding the alarm like *Chicken Little* with cries of, "The sky is falling, the sky is falling," when in reality what is falling is their faith in the ultimate victory of our Lord Jesus over all things!

- - - -

Starting and Finishing!

We all know that Christian parents of grown children still have great concern for their welfare, not just in terms of their health and prosperity but in their status with the Lord. When they were still living under dad and mom's roof, following them to Sunday school and church was the norm. When we thought they had caught their parent's faith in Jesus at a young age, we couldn't know then that some of them would later in life make some pretty awful mistakes and carry on in lifestyles that make us wonder if they ever genuinely met Jesus as Lord.

Many of those who heard Jesus spin out the parable of the prodigal son(s) could identify with the heartbroken father who had raised his boys to properly fear the Lord, yet both men had their ways of leaving their father and his God for a time. One left with his feet, the other left with his heart.

After an exchange of texts with a brother who has concerns for his grown son who supposedly "came to Jesus" long ago as a youngster, I felt the following message arise within me. Hope you too are blessed and edified:

- - - -

Well, you know how our hearts are capable of all kinds of reasoning. Maybe you will enjoy a certain true story.

A certain church decided to set up a week-long revival. Every night, the guest evangelist would bring a fine message, lifting up the Lord Jesus, followed by a lengthy altar call.

There was a lady in town that most folks knew. She was a nice lady, kind to her neighbors, never a troublemaker. But even though most of the townsfolk attended one of their local churches, this nice lady had never joined any of them.

One day, while reading her local newspaper, she noticed an ad that was promoting these seven nightly services. Something pricked her heart. Now curious, she planned on going over one evening.

Having never been a church-goer, she thought she had better enter about five minutes after the start time and then just plop down on the back row closest to the door. She figured that spot would be safe. What she didn't yet know was that the evangelist was quite capable of casting the seed of His Word all the way to the back row.

She heard him explain that "You may be a good person, but that isn't good enough for a perfect and Holy God." He told how God had made a way for us good yet flawed humans could have hope of being welcomed into His presence once we left this world.

On and on went this evangelist. Everything he was saying was like a punch in this nice lady's gut. By the time the invitation was given, she practically ran to the front and declared that she needed Jesus in her life. The evangelist led her in prayer to confess her sin and to receive Jesus as Lord. Then he told her that the baptistry was ready if she wanted to obey the Lord about getting baptized in His name. She eagerly agreed, and a deaconess led her to a back room where she changed into a simple white robe, and she got dunked. Then they offered her the Lord's supper of which she partook for the first time ever.

Once dried off and back into her own clothes, she was now almost the last one to leave the sanctuary. There she was, standing at the door, shaking the hand of the evangelist, and before she departed, she had one last serious question to ask him: "Now pastor, tell me, that is the end, isn't it?"

With marvelous wisdom, the evangelist smiled broadly and told her, "Yes mam, that is the *front* end!"

Any and all decisions to open one's life to invite Jesus to become their Lord and Savior are reason enough for rejoicing. But that is like rejoicing over the safe passage of a baby from the womb to the outside world. That is the front end. But now begins *lots* of work to raise and train those babes so they can grow up and know how to cope with this life for the next 70 or more years.

Multiple passages teach about the importance of going on with the Lord, not just making a start with the Lord. Here are a few from Hebrews:

Christ was faithful as a Son over His house whose house we are, **if we hold fast** our confidence and the boast of our hope **firm until the end**. (Heb. 3:6)

...Jesus became to all those **who obey Him** the source of eternal salvation.... (Heb. 5:9)

Pursue peace with all men, **and the sanctification without which no one will see the Lord**. (Heb. 12:14)

One of Christendom's greatest failures is the abandonment of newly born-again babes in Christ. We act as if just having a beginning with Jesus is enough. No, that is only the front end. You wouldn't leave your newborn baby on the front lawn of the hospital upon checkout where the child was born and then go home childless, expecting the baby left behind to thrive and grow up just fine.

As Simeon the priest said to Joseph and Mary when they brought Jesus to the Temple for dedication, "This child has been appointed for **the fall and rise** of many..." (Luke 2:34). Coming to Jesus begins with falling down before Him in humility and repentance. But after this beginning, then we learn to rise in Him **if we have spiritual fathers or mothers and big brothers or big sisters in the Lord who will feed us, watch over us, train us how to walk in Him, correct us, and so on**.

As Jesus said to Peter, "Feed my sheep" (John 21). If baby lambs are not fed, they are very weak and can easily perish.

A lady I knew who raised sheep told me something I have never forgotten since. In her sense of exasperation over two out of three newborn lambs who had just died soon after birth in spite of all her efforts to feed and care for them round the clock, she blurted out, "**Lambs are born looking for a place to die!**"

Getting born is the front end. Getting born again is also the front end. Oh may we who have made it past infancy awaken to our God-given responsibilities to care for the spiritual infants around us so they too can reach the back end in His presence forever!

- - - -

Prophets and Prophecies

A Texas friend and I were chatting today. Something he said prompted a memory, and then after he read my story, he had a question that pursued the ticklish question of modern-day prophets and prophecies. Hope you too are blessed by our exchange.

- - - -

That reminds me of a time when I was teaching in an Indonesian Bible school about various prophecies, one of which is about the upcoming mark of the Beast to be put into one's right hand or forehead. So I asked the class why the forehead, and I waited for any replies or guesses. None came forth. But they were looking at me very eagerly, expecting some great revelation about what the forehead does mean.

So I just raised my right arm with my hand folded back so that from their perspective, it would appear like I had no right hand, and I simply said, “Because some people don’t have a right hand, but everyone does have a forehead.”

About two heartbeats passed… and then they died laughing!

- - - -

He replied,

“😜 Clever indeed.”

- - - -

Well, my comment was based upon my observations that while most humans do indeed have two hands, a few I have met only have one hand. But how could you have a live conscious human who had no forehead?

So moral of the story is that when seeking for understanding, it is not always necessary to “dig deep” and come up with some gnostic-style secret knowledge. How often do you suppose that the simplest explanation is probably the best and most accurate interpretation to draw? Hmm?

- - - -

He wrote back:

“Hmm…

On another topic, what is your opinion of modern prophets? We just went through an end-times class at church where the teacher drew more from them than from the Bible!!"

- - - -

I always remind folks that there is one very significant difference between me and the Holy Spirit, and that is the trait called forgetfulness. I can ask someone their name, and gee whiz, only two seconds after he or she tells me, I find that I have already forgotten that name.

But the Holy Spirit inspired the writing of the entire book called *The Bible*. And He does *not* forget any jot, tittle, or iota that is in there.

So whenever teaching on predictive prophecies, if the one teaching seems pretty thin in his knowledge of the Scriptures and instead just goes with "freshly inspired words of knowledge to forecast upcoming events," my feeling is that that teacher is proving how lazy he is by neglecting to study The Book from cover to cover so that when a lesson is taught, the hearers see for themselves how much Scripture there is to support the predictions and conclusions that are brought forth.

This is quite the anomaly in charismatic Christendom overall, in my opinion. We say that we believe in the person, the works, the signs and wonders, and the various manifestations which come forth from the Holy Spirit. Fine. But why would the Spirit who inspired The Book now instead lead God's Spirit-filled people *away* from The Book instead of *toward* The Book?!

As I heard Malcolm Smith (a Pentecostal servant from England) say once, "As far as I am concerned, the attesting sign that someone has been filled with the Spirit is that he will wear out a Bible."

Or as the two-line poem affirms:

"Bibles that are falling apart
Are usually owned by people who aren't."

I like and quote that one often! If someone teaches about *prophecies* without much connection to the Scriptures, then that would be like a school teacher who gives the students a test. Once filled in and turned over to the teacher, what does she do next? She must grade each test. How? By pulling out the test key and checking side by side each student's answers with that of the key to mark each one correct or wrong. But what if there were no key? How would those test answers be checked whether they were right or wrong?

Scripture is our test key. We check on any and all modern *prophecies* by comparing those items one by one with the test key. If we cannot find much or anything to support those things, then we must do what Paul said, "Do not quench the Spirit; do not despise prophetic utterances. But

examine everything carefully; hold fast to that which is good" (1 Thess. 5:19–21).

If you care to dig into three chapters, I have noticed that Jer. 27, 28, and 29 all deal with this matter of various *prophets* who indeed were not ordained by Heaven, and thus what they prophesied were only lies. Look at how serious this matter is to the Lord. One named Hananiah was judged, and within two months of hearing from Jeremiah that the Lord condemned him for "causing this people to trust in a lie," he was dead (Jer. 28:1, 15–17).

Two more false prophets who were among the Jewish exiles in Babylon named Ahab and Zedekiah were arrested by King Nebuchadnezzar and sentenced to be roasted alive on a spit over a raging fire. Care for any barbecued false prophet? (Jer. 29:21–23)

Another prophecy by one called Shemaiah were equated with "rebellion against the Lord." So the Heavenly consequence that would come down upon him was that his entire lineage would no longer be found among God's people (Jer. 29:24–32).

I am not in agreement with certain denominational stances which declare that there are no more offices of prophet or apostle after those died off in the first century of the church. Where can such an edict in Scripture be found which predicts such a cessation of those kinds of ministry gifts to His body?

Oh sure, I have heard of such an attempt by those who turn to the Love Chapter as they quote the following: "Love never fails; but if there are gifts of prophecy, they will be done away; if there are tongues, they will cease; if there is knowledge, it will be done away. For we know in part, and we prophesy in part; **but when the perfect comes, the partial will be done away**" 1 Cor. 13:8–10).

Fine, so tell me, who is the perfect One? That would be Jesus. And has He come back the second time yet? No? Well then, apparently He isn't finished with the ministry offices of apostles (which means, "sent ones," i.e., *missionaries*) and prophets either.

So my hope is that we make room in our hearts for modern-day prophets to be allowed to fulfill their ministries. But we must keep in mind that all of God's servants are still a work in progress. None of us are 100% perfect quite yet.

So when we discern that a certain prophesy is not well grounded upon His written Word, I hope we will have the same good sense that the Lord gave to cows as they graze in a field of grass. When they run into some twigs down in the grass, what do they do? Those bovines just nose them to one side and continue feeding upon the bright green blades of the pasture.

- - - -

He finished with, "My thoughts exactly but I could not state it so well!"

- - - -

To Acquire a Second Tongue

After a friend in Virginia listened to the three-minute clip that a pastor's wife recorded a week ago when I brought the message in Malay/Indo lingo, she texted me, "Cool to hear you in their language. I'm amazed."

So I sent back the testimony of how the Lord worked out this accomplishment in my life. Hope you are blessed:

- - - -

May the Lord get all the credit for that linguistic breakthrough. By and large, other people of this world are known for picking up multiple languages, but not us Americans.

Have you heard the joke that at first doesn't sound like a joke, just a series of questions?

What do you call someone who can speak three languages? Answer: trilingual.

What do you call someone who can speak two languages? Answer: bilingual.

What do you call someone who can only speak one language?

Answer: American.

My first year overseas (June 1986–September 1987) was based in Medan in North Sumatra, Indonesia. Due to the failure at that point of not acquiring a long-term Visa for that nation, I had to pack up and shift next door to Penang, Malaysia.

Most of the flocks who were opening doors for me in this area were functioning in English (since this land used to be called British Malaya). So I thought, "Why am I struggling any longer with trying to break into Indonesian?" So I took my Alkitab (the Indonesian Bible) and put it on a shelf in my Penang home.

But about a month later, I heard the Lord say, "Go get your Alkitab." Oh, ok.

So for the next seven years, I had my daily quiet time with two Bibles open in front of me, English on the right, Indonesian on the left. Verse by verse, back and forth, my eyes would scan through every passage of Scripture in both lingos. In this way, the Lord continued to build up my vocabulary.

After doing this for five years, the Lord opened a door for me to enter and serve in an island of Indonesia which I had heard about since I moved there in 1986 called Nias. It is just west of the province of North Sumatra.

Three pastors who each headed up three denominations on Nias gladly welcomed me and my friend (Benjamin) from Medan who came to function as my interpreter whenever bringing messages at their services if invited. But while the five of us would sit and drink coffee and chat, I was capable enough to speak back and forth with them in Indonesian.

But once Ben and I stepped into their pulpits together, me speaking in English and Ben interpreting into Indonesian, those pastors made a request of me. They explained that they had members who only knew the local Nias language and had never become fluent in the national lingo called Indonesian. Since they thought I knew enough Indonesian, they asked if I could please try to bring messages in that tongue, and the Nias pastor would act as my interpreter into the Nias language.

I didn't feel very confident that I could do that yet, but I conceded to give it a try. Well, I look back now and see it as another of God's stepping stones to get me moved into direct usage of that language in ministry. By having three trips to Nias from 1992 to 1994, it was a middle step whereby I could utter one statement in Indonesian, and while the Nias pastor would be interpreting it, I could be thinking how to utter the next sentence.

Then came graduation day, or I should say, graduation fortnight in March of 1994. Ben and I had supposedly lined up two weeks of travels and service together around four areas of Sumatra. But when I flew over to Medan on a Friday and then called Ben to ask if he was ready to leave with me on the morrow to start our plan together, he was shocked to hear my voice on the phone.

Why? Because he thought the plan was to happen starting on the 18th of April, the next month, not the 18th of March. But I had already called each contact in those areas, and I knew that they were expecting me for dates in March, not April. So it was Benjamin who messed up, not me.

So Ben told me that he already had other ministry plans and that he could not go with me to serve together. That meant I had to get into a charter taxi without any interpreter and head off to do services and seminars for two weeks with no fluent interpreter standing beside me. After a five-hour ride to Tarutung, I then checked into a little hotel on Saturday night. The next day, I entered a pulpit twice, with knocking knees, yet everyone present understood those messages. Then Monday to Wednesday, four hours a day, I taught the Godly Leadership Seminar for the first time ever, with fourteen Bible school students and two local pastors present, and they understood!

The entire two weeks of ministry, I had no interpreter, and they understood. Once I flew back to Penang, I said to myself,

"How about that? By His grace, I have now graduated." Since then 'til now, I no longer seek out an interpreter for Malay/ Indo contexts of ministry. Hallelujah! To Him be all the glory.

- - - -

Scripture and Prayer

Have you noticed how Christendom tends to have a certain emphasis but not always the same emphasis? One sector proclaims vigorously for how much we need the Scriptures, while the other sector says that we need more prayer and intercession. But this should not be an either-or situation. Both are true. We need the Book, *and* we need to keep each other lifted up to His throne of grace.

A brother in Oklahoma reached me a few days ago, kinda discouraged about so much bad news in the world today. I felt prompted to send him the following testimony about how much more I need His messages than those which arise from secular sources. Here's how our exchange went:

- - - -

As much as I loved and appreciated a conservative news commentator for his wisdom and insight, I can also admit that there were times when I awoke to smell the coffee. I realized that all of his witty commentary was not actually giving any relief to my troubled soul over so much bad news on so many fronts.

That's when I recognized that I must use some discipline **and turn off the radio and laptop from listening so much to those sources of news.**

Us fretting over bad news will not help us maintain peace of heart. So we must obey Jesus once again and do those three little words He spoke:

Come to Me

Because He is alive and not just a famous figure way back in history, then we can do that. We can come to Him, spend more time with Him, listen to Him, pour out to Him all of our burdens and concerns, and then wait—wait in His presence for what He will do or say or both in our lives.

When our souls get weary, coming to Jesus in a fresh way is the only solution I know of so that new strength and peace of mind are restored unto us. As David said, "He (the Lord, the Good Shepherd) restores my soul" (Psalm 23:3).

So check the gauge on the status of what fills your heart and how much of it you now have. Is the needle toward "full" on the amount of peace that is within you? Or is the needle pointing to the big "E" meaning almost empty?

He is ready to refill your tank up to the top with His peace, and the price per gallon has never changed. Just pay with your simple faith unto obedience (Rom. 1:5 and 16:26).

- - - -

He wrote back to say he had mostly stopped watching and listening to secular news since a few years ago. So I added a bit more to our chat.

- - - -

That's half of the solution. (He replied, "Staying in the Word is the other half. Amen.")

Yep… but don't let it become an academic thing. It isn't just a book full of truths. It is a sign post directing you to the One who is its Author, He Himself being the Truth.

- - - -

A day later, the same brother asked me to lift up his sister in prayer about an urgent medical need, which I did. Then a memory came back to me, which I passed along to him about the importance of praying one for another. Here's what I sent him.

- - - -

Back in my college days, while I lived in the dorm for four years, a Christian friend of mine and I met in the hallway. So we asked each other, "Where you going now?" I said I was headed to a Bible study. He said he was headed to a prayer meeting.

After I heard his reply, I repeated it out loud, with that tone of voice that kinda said I didn't think that was a very good use of time. My friend recognized my disparaging tone, and he looked me in the eye and said something I have never since forgotten.

He simply smiled and said, "If we Christians don't pray for one another, no one else will either."

This world is full of people who pray, but can you imagine when you have a certain burden that you see a son of Ishmael heading into his place of worship on a Friday and then asking him, "Say, while you're in there, would you please pray for me?" They don't pray for us. They pray against us!

Or how about the Hindu heading into his nearby temple full of idols. Can you see yourself asking him to intercede for you while he is in there going through his rituals? He is praying to demons. Do you want more or less attention from demons?

Or how about the Buddhist who dutifully burns the joss incense sticks while praying to their dead relatives who they believe will become gods through the worship of the living ones still upon this earth. Can you see yourself requesting one of them to pray for your problem? Will their prayers do you any good?

How about those who pray to Mary or to one of the saints, fervently using their Rosary beads and kneeling before statues and burning candles? Would their prayers help your situation at all?

As my friend boldly said, "If we Christians don't pray for one another, no one else will."

- - - -

Our counsel and exhortation to our brethren needs to be Scripture and prayer, not one *or* the other.

- - - -

Protecting the Sheep

I awoke to find this text from a fellow servant in Vietnam, a nation where I have not yet gone in person. He sent me this:

"Dear friends, please lift me up in your prayers. My heart has been really troubled for over a week knowing that some members of our church now follow Jehovah's Witness."

Like Paul who would send letters to churches which he himself had not founded, I too have felt urged from above to mix my hand in matters where I sense that His counsel is very much needed. I hope you too are blessed and edified by the following message and testimony:

- - - -

My brother,

I know we have not yet met each other in person. Maybe the Lord will open a door for that to happen later this year or next. Anyone who is called to serve in fields far from home knows that we need more normalcy to be restored in the travel industry and in reductions of onerous restrictions placed upon travelers by the governments of this world. The Covid excuse must die off first.

But at least I can reach you via WhatsApp with what I hope will be counsel from above. Since I got up late today, and then checked for messages, yours has touched my heart strings. So I have sat for a while, thinking of you and of your difficult situation concerning some "members" in your flock who have turned unto the teachings of the cult of the JWs.

I will try to keep this reply brief. But frankly, whole books have been composed on the matters of various cults and their false doctrines.

Yet what I ask you to consider is this: what is it that made those *members* so open and vulnerable to the persuasions of those ideas from that cult? The antidote to false doctrines is true doctrines. The majority of orthodox doctrines of classical Christianity are found and rooted in our three primary books of doctrine, called Romans, Galatians, and Hebrews. But if the lessons that any flock hears each week are very light in the matter of sound doctrine, then that absence creates **an unholy opportunity** for our enemy to come along by way of false apostles who teach very strongly their own perversions of the Scriptures concerning foundational beliefs.

Please ask the Lord to help you think through what kinds of messages you have been giving to your flock. As Jesus said, the mouth speaks from what fills the heart (Luke 6:45). So, is your heart full, or only half full, or maybe just got a few drops in it of the sound doctrines of our faith which are found in those three parts of our New Testament?

As Jesus said, let him without sin cast the first stone. I have no place to judge you, my brother, even though what I am asking you to do may seem like I am laying the responsibility at your feet for those members going astray into false ideas.

But I know my own story. Though I was born into a pastor's family and was raised in all church activities, I was quite vulnerable in my teen years to the persuasions of a very ungodly philosophy. How did it happen? Oh, it all seemed innocent enough.

On my sixteenth birthday, several friends were invited to my house where Mom cooked up a special dinner for my gang. After the birthday cake was served, I was handed several gifts to open. One of them was a novel by Ayn Rand called *The Fountainhead*. It was a paperback of over 700 pages.

But it was not just a fictional story to entertain the readers. The author used her creativity to preach her kind of philosophy through her protagonists, which held to the ideas called "the virtue of selfishness," while she contrasted her positions with obvious antagonist characters who held what were called altruistic views. And of course, by the end of the book, the self-centered ones were the victorious heroes.

If you wonder how in the world could a preacher's teenage kid be persuaded to buy into all of Ayn's ideas, then let me confess what my church background was very weak in. When it came to any kind of doctrinal orientation toward Christianity, I was taught almost nothing but one simple truth, which was "God is love."

Yes, that is true, but He is much more than only love. He is also Holy, and by contrast, I am not holy. I am lost in my sin and in desperate need of His saving grace which comes to repentant sinners who say yes and amen to the substitutionary death of Jesus upon His cross in my place, a place that I richly deserve, but by His mercy, I don't have to die in my sin. I can be saved unto eternal life by receiving the living resurrected Jesus as my Lord.

But what I have just written here I frankly did not clearly know when I was sixteen from all my years raised in church. And that lack of sound doctrinal teaching left me wide open to the persuasive books that Ayn Rand produced which were rich in her particular philosophy. I now thank the Lord that over the next few years, He reached my mind with the many truths in Scripture which became the antidote for the poison of those false ideas I had swallowed.

So again, my brother and fellow servant, I just ask you to pray asking the Lord to help you to assess your teaching ministry with brutal honesty. If proper doctrinal teaching has been missing, then this has created opportunities for false ideas to be planted in your member's minds whenever the cults come along to befriend and persuade your people with their strong convictions but wrong conclusions.

But our Lord can make you strong where formerly you were weak. By the ninth fruit of His Spirit, you can exercise self-control so that you become a man of The Book, **the whole Book**, including the richness of the doctrinal parts which are absolutely necessary as a solid foundation for all of His saints. That is how we protect our sheep.

- - - -

Parallels (Exodus 7–14 and Revelation 17–19)

What has happened before may soon come again! The Lord is opening my eyes to notice parallels between the days and ministry of Moses with the end-time predictions that could be fulfilled in our lifetimes. But don't just take my word for it. Double-check all of the following Scripture references for yourself:

- - - -

The pharaoh says he does not know the Lord, thus he won't listen to a message from the Lord, that is, to let His people go. So… (Exod. 5:1 and 2).

God introduces Himself, by way of the following signs… (Exod. 7–12).

Moses' staff becomes a snake then changes back to a wooden staff. (Please take note that this sign does *not* cause any great loss or suffering either to the pharaoh nor to His people, so it is not one of the following ten things called plagues or curses.) (Exod. 7:8–13)

…the Nile turns to blood (Exod. 7:14–25).

…the land overflows with frogs (8:1–15).

…dust becomes gnats (Exod. 8:16–19).

…swarms of insects afflict only Egyptian households (Exod. 8:20–32).

…deadly disease sent upon only Egyptian livestock (Exod. 9:1–7).

…sore boils break out upon the Egyptians and their beasts (Exod. 9:8–12).

…a heavy fall of hail kills men, beasts, and plants in the open fields (Exod. 9:13–35).

…swarms of locusts devour trees and plants that still remained (Exod. 10:1–20).

…darkness falls over all of Egypt (except where the Hebrews dwell) for three full days so none of the Egyptians can move around or function (Exod. 10:21–29).

…the death angel strikes down the first born of Egypt's people and cattle but passes over the Hebrew's homes marked by the blood of a slain lamb, and the Hebrews plunder the wealth of the Egyptians who are now in dread of the Hebrews and their God (Exod. 11 and 12:35, 36).

…the Hebrews cross the Red Sea by the miraculous opening of the sea. When the Egyptian army tries to do so, the waters close upon them drowning the entire army (Exod. 14:1–31).

So how does the order of these events parallel to what is predicted at the last days?

Revelation 17 reveals the coming judgment upon the mother of harlots, harlots being the various religions of this world. The Egyptians had a variety of idols and things which they worshiped. According to Numbers 33:3 and 4, the Lord had "executed judgments upon the gods of Egypt." So the first four plagues or curses that visited upon Egypt (after the first demonstration of miraculous power by Moses' staff becoming a snake) were divine actions directed against what the Egyptians worshiped, that is, the Nile, frogs, and creatures from the insect world.

Revelation 18 reveals the coming judgment against the corrupt business world. Starting in Exod. 9 through chapter 12, the next six judgments all adversely affect the entire Egyptian economy. In fact, the prophet Zechariah also gave several predictions concerning end-times matters, including some features of the 1000-year rule of Jesus upon the earth. The last such prophecy is found at Zech. 14:16–21, and the very last line foretells that "…there will no longer be a Canaanite (see margin note, i.e., a merchant or a businessman) in the house of the Lord of hosts in that day." The business world's bottom line is all about money, profit, and greed, and that is why it is a worthy candidate for the Lord's judgment in the last days, that is, as we see in Rev. 18.

Revelation 19:11–21 reveals the coming judgment against the governments of this world, including their militaries. What happens in Exod. 14 when the Lord opened the sea for His people to escape and then the Lord closed the sea over His people's enemies which was the government of Egypt and its army parallels to what is predicted to happen when Jesus mounts His horse and leads the army of Heaven to battle against the Antichrist, the false prophet, and those armies who follow them.

So it seems to me that there are indeed parallels both in activity and in sequential order found at both ends of The Book. In order to set God's people free from all kinds of bondage, the Lord must do the following:

1. Get us out of religions and into a living relationship with Him through Jesus as Lord.

2. Get us out of the worldly system of how to prosper ourselves and into a reliance upon His ways to conduct ourselves in relation to one another in full honesty and fairness.

3. Get our eyes off of the political kingdoms of this world for righting the wrongs around us and instead look unto His coming Kingdom where everything will be just and true.

As John said at the end of The Book, I hope we join him to say, "Maranatha! Amen. Come, Lord Jesus!" (Rev. 22:20).

- - - -

Next!

A pastor friend here in Southeast Asia just reached me with news and a question. He said that in a few months, he will retire at the age of sixty-four. So he asked me if I knew of anyone to possibly become the next shepherd of his flock. Here's how I fielded that one, and I hope this also gives you food for thought:

- - - -

Well, if you are open to take a page out of the early church playbook, back then there were no seminary or Bible school degrees to acquire first before one was ordained into various ministries. Instead they followed the example of Jesus who had two kinds of ministry, what I call public ministry *and* private ministry.

Public ministry meant that Jesus would preach and witness (to the lost, in groups or one on one), teach (the saved), and counsel (the confused), plus heal the sick and cast out demons by holy authority.

Note: Ever since He showed me the importance of Deut. 23:14, I can no longer just say that the believer has authority over our enemy **if we allow unholiness into our lives**. But if our holy God is indeed in our camp, then we will indeed have **holy authority** to cast out evil spirits.

But private ministry meant that Jesus called certain men to become close followers of Him. At one point, Scripture says He had as many as seventy that He would send out two by two to go and practice ministry, not just the twelve. And inside of the twelve, three of them got even more personal attention, Peter, James, and John. And among these three, one was told that Jesus would give him the keys to the Kingdom, Peter.

These kinds of men in His private ministry were mentored by Jesus to do the following:

1. Listen to God's Word from Jesus, not just what He taught publicly but extra time spent hearing Him explain the meanings of His parables.

2. Witness His example. Jesus demonstrated how to walk out His ministry.

As Solomon said, "A slave will not be instructed by words alone, for though he understands (those words), he will not act" (Prov. 29:19). This begs the question, "Why not?" And in my opinion, there are three plausible answers, which are as follows:

A. Laziness

B. Rebelliousness

C. Fear—of what? Of not being sure you can do something without first witnessing a good example to **show you how it's done**.

Which of those three reasons is the main culprit? I reckon the answer is C.

In the villages of Indonesia, I have seen a variety of real water wells. I never saw one in America except for wishing wells at the zoo where you'd pitch in a penny and make a wish.

If, one day, someone handed me a shovel and ordered me to make a new water well, what's my reaction? I am hesitant to just start digging a hole because I know a real water well is much more than a hole in the ground. So am I lazy or rebellious toward this instruction? Not really.

It is fear that stops me because so far in my life, no one has ever shown me how to make a functional water well. But if a skilled worker will let me become his assistant so I can watch and learn from his words and his example while we work side by side to produce that well, then my confidence grows that someday, I can make another well all by myself.

So Jesus' disciples used their ears to listen to all that Jesus would teach and explain, their eyes to notice His excellent example in how to walk things out, and their own hands and feet to be sent out by Jesus from time to time to go practice ministry and then come back and report to Jesus how things went (Luke 9:1–6, 10).

Our modern training centers usually only imitate the first one. They teach, teach, teach much truth. But the second and third things that Jesus did for His men are rarely or lightly done at all these days.

This is how the early church trained and prepared the next batch of leaders. They trusted the Lord for Timothy's to mentor in a personal way.

Today when I ask any pastor what seems like a simple question, they are often stumped or baffled as to my meaning. That question is, "Who is your Timothy here?" Everyone knows the name Timothy, but the concept of at least one soul among those brethren being the pastor's current Timothy seems like a strange idea.

Frankly, I feel that if the Haggai prophecy is going to be fulfilled that the latter glory of God's house will exceed the former (Hag. 2:9), this isn't going to happen while we rely upon highly academic training centers to produce for His church the next crop of leaders that we need. Methinks we need to reexamine what Jesus did, and the early church did, who did far more than produce scholars. They produced real shepherds and evangelists and church planters and missionaries **by mentoring them**.

So, my brother, please take someone under your wing, like Moses did for Joshua and Caleb; like Elijah did for Elisha; like Barnabas did for Paul and for John Mark; and like Paul did for Silas, Timothy, Titus, and many others during his ministry. That's the one who should fill your shoes when He moves you on to other ministry or into His presence.

- - - -

Post-July 4th Musings

Can I ask you what may seem like a silly question?

When a parade of US citizens who cast themselves as America-haters hit the airwaves and the Internet with threats to leave the country because it is so awful nowadays, does anyone besides me want to reply to them with "do you need help packing?" or "I can give you a ride to the airport"?

Frankly I have a solution for all those naysayers and malcontents. Years ago, I read that Indonesia has as many as 17,000 islands. But that wasn't the real kicker. It was the follow-up statement, which said "almost 300 of those islands have people on them."

?!?

Simple math says that means there are thousands of islands that if each malcontent were sent to one of those spots on the map, now that island would have a population of one!

Then wouldn't America be a much happier place to live? Less noise. Less complaining. Less rebellion.

The old bumper sticker comes to mind…

America. Love it, or leave it!

- - - -

Was Tom Hanks a very contented and happy camper while supposedly being stranded on a deserted island for four years in the story called *Cast Away*? Why did that character keep trying to escape that Island? Why was he grateful to eventually get back to America even if his wife had now married another man, assuming he had died in that air crash at sea? Why so if America is such an awful place?

- - - -

And what is the one simple refutation on the idea that America is so awful?

Daily the invasion of illegals by the thousands continue to cross America's southern border!

Why so if the United States is such a hellhole?!

- - - -

People who are determined to complain cannot be deterred.

To illustrate, I love repeating the following story about the hard-to-please hubby. Goes like this…

One morning, a man's wife fixed for his breakfast two fried eggs. He sat down, looked at his plate, and grumbled, "Today I wanted scrambled."

So the next day, she fixed for him two scrambled eggs. He looked at his plate and said, "Today I wanted fried."

So the next day she fixed him one fried egg and one scrambled egg. He looked at his plate and fussed, "You scrambled the wrong one!"

Hercule Poirot Never Dies

A brother in Oklahoma and I carried on a chat today. He hopes that the Lord will soon use his counsel and his love to help two others that he deals with regularly to cease from strife and return to a harmonious relationship. I commended him for this and added the following Scriptural reminder:

"Blessed are the peacemakers for they shall be called sons of God."

He replied with, "The greatest blessings the Lord bestows on me is when He uses me as His conduit."

This prompted me to send the following message, to which he had a sobering reply. I hope you too are blessed and strengthened by our exchange:

- - - -

Have you occasionally read some novels? I have noticed that a certain feature of most novels is a certain spot near the end of the book where the hero figure has a monologue in which all of the previous mysteries in the overall story finally get revealed and all questions are finally answered, such as, it was Colonel Mustard in the library who used the pipe wrench to clobber the sad victim. But more than that, even the answer as to why he did it comes to light through our hero, such as Hercule Poirot, the Belgian detective created by the mind of Agatha Christie.

And of course the hero acquires even more glory and admiration from all parties, even from the hero's detractors, for how clever the mind of the hero is to have solved all these things. The hero might even ride off into the sunset with a great reward for such fine sleuthing.

But then I compare those fictional heroes with Biblical heroes, real men and real women of God Almighty who truly lived upon the earth, and how God gave them great insight so that they knew just what to say even in the face of great opposition and strife. Stephen is one such man.

But the sobering thing about being the right man for the right time with the exact right words to speak out clearly can result in the opposite of love and admiration. I have just read again Acts 7 which contains Stephen's one recorded message. We "listen" to his words of defense which were actually God's offense against those who thus far opposed the gospel message and the spread of His churches. It's a worthy study to go over that entire monologue.

But does his message result in the hearers becoming humbled to the point of repentance? Quite the opposite. Instead they are humiliated into nothing more than an angry mob who gnashes their teeth at Stephen followed by turning into screeching banshees who drag him out of the Temple where he was on trial. Then they stoned him to death. If you can't refute the message, just kill the messenger. That was Stephen's "reward."

So in real life, God's obedient heroes do not always garner admiration for their great and insightful messages. But we also know that Stephen got more than a "well done" from His Lord upon arrival at the Pearly Gates of Heaven. He also got the exquisite joy of being the second in line to greet another newcomer to Heaven a few years later (the first Welcomer is always Jesus), for when Paul walked into His holy Presence and was hugged by the Almighty, guess who was standing right behind Him? I am sure it was Stephen. What a reunion that was! What things those two must have shared back and forth. What a different man Paul had become soon after he had participated in the martyrdom of Stephen.

So yes, let's all be encouraged that we too who follow Jesus as Lord can become channels of truth, wisdom, and insight from above. But unlike fictional heroes, we too may face scorn and hostility from folks who do not immediately repent of their foolish thoughts nor their ungodly ways after they hear those blessed words come out of our mouths.

- - - -

He sent back, “I had a vision some years ago that I would be a martyr for Christ. I pray for His strength if that’s true.”

So I added the following:

- - - -

Brother, between salvation (which for most folks happens in their younger years) and crossing over into His glorious Presence (which usually is decades later), there are *lots* of opportunities to put into practice the lessons of the Lord. We are to learn to love one another. We become givers not just once but over and over. We have many occasions to forgive, not just seven times but seventy times seven and beyond.

But there is one thing that we cannot practice over and over. We cannot practice martyrdom. If called upon to have that be our last witness for the Lord, how do we know we can face that threat and then faithfully lay down our earthly lives in a way that is pleasing to our Lord?

We just look again at Stephen. The last two things we learn from his story before he breathes his last is that he shows us the living Lord Jesus rising up on the inside of him, making possible that glorious exit from this life. “Lord, don’t hold this sin against them.” That’s like Jesus on the cross praying, “Father, forgive them, for they know not what they do.” And lastly Stephen uttered, “Lord, receive my spirit.” Jesus from the cross prayed, “Father, into Your hands I commit my Spirit.”

Let's make it a practice of staying close to Jesus daily when there are no threats or hostility against us just now. Then surely we shall experience His closeness if or when our time of laying down this life has come in the face of mortal peril.

- - - -

He replied with, "This is what I do, my brother."Amen. Me too.

- - - -

The Axe: Sharp or Dull?

Once again, my work proves that receiving brief texts with a short question necessitate a thoughtful reply that isn't so brief. For those who have wondered about going on a mission trip or considering short-term cross-cultural work, take a peek into my world from the following exchange. Hope you are blessed:

- - - -

Hello Doug. We have a young man who has a heart for Thailand. He is looking for a ministry there who could host him for a couple months to minister to the people, do evangelism, and so on.

Would you know anyone there you could recommend?

- - - -

Well, some things to consider.

Unlike Malaysia or Singapore, Thailand has never been under the British. Therefore the amount of English known by their population at large is rather minimal, with even less being known in more rural settings. The amount of time needed for the typical Westerner to acquire sufficient conversational language skills in Thai is two years. Without such, your young man friend would be in constant need of an interpreter beside him.

I don't have a lot of personal contacts in that nation. But besides getting himself flown over to Bangkok, what does this fella expect from a host family? Will he come with sufficient means to cover his daily expenses for that entire sixty days? Or is he asking to become someone's guest for that whole time? Has he researched yet to learn how much moola he would need to be self-supporting?

He also needs to know about what the restrictions are that will be placed upon him upon arrival and dealing with immigration vis-à-vis the whole Covid mess. If they demand that he first be jabbed once or twice before being allowed entry, that could become a debacle before he's even allowed entrance to the nation.

Any host for him is going to need an understanding with the youngster that he MUST clear his intended activities that are done in public and/or in existing gatherings of the saints with his hosts. Otherwise he literally can endanger the longevity of the long-termer by his actions that lead to terrible repercussions not just for the short-term youngster.

How much language acquisition activity is he willing to engage in before ever setting up his air tickets to/from Thailand? Where does he live now? If in a large enough metropolitan city, then he can find Thai expats who own, run, and work at Thai-style restaurants. Then he can find some of those Thai folks to befriend and to seek their help so he can begin to practice his Thai skills in communication. Tell him to check out the LAMP course: Language Acquisition Made Practical.

He can also test the waters by eating some of the typical spicy dishes at those restaurants to see if he's been given the stomach to handle those flavors at that level of heat!

Any potential host will want to know this young man's testimony of salvation and about where he is at in terms of growth and discipleship since getting saved. They will want to hear from him, both in writing and orally, in order to gain some insight as to his level of maturity. They will also want to hear from the youngster's significant others in his life, such as his pastor, parents, Bible school teachers, and so on.

What ministry and/or mission trip experience does he already have? You mentioned evangelism. Before he ever attempts such cross-culturally, what has he done in personal soul winning in his original context and culture? What has he done *after* anyone has prayed with him to receive Jesus as Lord?

Has he then done proper follow-up to disciple that new convert? Or has he just moved on to the next scalp?

He may think that I am just trying to discourage him from taking baby steps into fields abroad. But I am just being realistic, in light of my thirty-six years of experience in His service. As an older servant (who had lived in and served in two East African nations for many years) told me when I was in my twenties, "Time spent sharpening the axe is *not* wasted time."

So yes, what all I have laid out here would indeed be time-consuming. But it would also be time well spent if he is serious about getting launched into foreign service for our Lord Jesus, short term or longer.

- - - -

THE AXE (PART 2)

After a brother in Oklahoma read my last article called "The Axe: Sharp or Dull?", he wrote back saying, "Interesting insight. Makes complete sense, but I had no idea of the preparation required."

Frankly I had only shown the tip of the iceberg to him as to what practical steps I myself had gone through in order to be commissioned into work overseas for our Lord. So I composed the following, and I hope this testimony blesses your heart also:

- - - -

Between the time in my last year of seminary (1979–1980) when the Lord twisted the dial on the side of the microscope and brought into sharper focus what my calling to become His servant meant (which was missions abroad, not state-side-shepherding a local flock as my dad did full-time for thirty-eight years before he dropped back to part-time interim ministry for several years as he entered retirement), so by

June of 1980, I somewhat hesitantly relented and said yes, do you know when it was that I did finally begin full-time service with Indonesia being my first overseas home? It was June... **of 1986!**

The Lord worked on me for six more years, sharpening the axe, before finally opening that door to leave one side of the world and shift my whole family to the other side. During those six years, He moved me around the country, from Texas to Illinois and later to California, then to Missouri, and then back to Texas.

I had to leave one agency that I had followed their guidelines for four years as preparatory toward field work abroad because they could no longer assure me of obtaining a long-term Visa for dwelling in Indonesia where the Lord had specifically told me to go first. Then He led me to Omega in the spring of 1984, and I have been with them ever since.

I took the LAMP course (Language Acquisition Made Practical) in the summer of 1982 while fulfilling three months of specialty classes designed just for missionary candidates at the School of World Missions at Fuller Theological Seminary in Pasadena, California. That was the beginning of me picking up Indonesian language from Indonesians who now called Los Angeles their home. Some of them gave me their used books which had helped them to learn English better. So I reverse engineered those books to help me learn more Indonesian.

Then two years were spent building the original support base. He had to show me guiding principles along my way in His Word to make that happen.

To tell you the truth, until that time period, I had never known there were so many ways to say "no" until enough churches or individual believers would make commitments so that two budgets could be raised, one sustaining budget and one send-off budget.

The worst way that I could be told "no" was when they actually said "yes," which thrilled heart, only to prove later that their yes really meant no and they would not follow through on those supposed pledges. But the Lord faithfully helped me make progress on both budgets, yet it was not an overnight wonder.

And why did it take two years to build the original support base? Consider the following story:

To illustrate the difficulty to raise up a support base even in the midst of American Christendom (which indeed has a reputation worldwide as a generous church), consider this. A pastor in little Tulia, Texas, agreed to give me an appointment to come chat with him.

But during that visit, he was much more interested in telling me what his flock was already doing to support world missions than in getting to know me.

And would you care to guess what they were doing for cross-cultural work elsewhere in the world? Well, apparently that shepherd had convinced his flock that they needed to finance him and his wife every year to go on a two-week "missions trip" (not a vacation, mind you) to where? To Rural Mexico? To Guyana in South America? Or to the Navajo Indian reservations in nearby New Mexico state? Nope to all of those.

That modest-sized church paid all of their expenses for the two of them to fly over **to Australia** and preach at a few services! Now don't get me wrong. I know that nation is largely agnostic, with only 5% of its population ever darkening the doorway of anything that calls itself "church." So yes, mission outreach is needed there.

But Australia is also a first world modern Western nation. So not too likely that anyone sent there in His service is going to deal with any poverty or difficult logistics or quite humble dwellings or strange foods.

You can imagine why that pastor then never extended any invitation for me to come and serve his flock. Why not? Because I would have become a competitor with him for their giving to missions. Guess who would have lost that battle? A field-based full-time missionary sent to a third world nation trumps a once-a-year 2-week "missions trip" (?) such as that couple enjoyed. Shenanigans like this story describes have happened all over the United States. Sigh.

Like I have said many times, when Moses was allowed to see the backside of the Lord as He passed by, it was still a glorious experience. But when you need a support base from His flocks in your homeland, you are going to see the backside of the churches, **and that ain't a very pretty sight**.

That's the price I paid and the path I had to follow to get ready for His service abroad. On this topic, I think I have earned the right to be heard.

And one more thing.

When it comes to Westerners and their penchant for heading overseas on so-called short-term mission trips, sometimes it is nothing more than "spiritual tourism." They are going on an adventure that seems quite exotic before they ever leave their home turf.

But that "glory-glory" shine will wear off pretty quickly once you get your feet upon foreign terra firma. So you'd better be there because truly He has sent you and prepared you for service instead of just looking around and taking photos of strange looking scenes and customs.

- - - -

NEXT! (PART 2)

After a pastor friend in the KL area reached me a few weeks ago about news of his upcoming retirement, if you read my reply, it was titled "Next!" as he was concerned about who would become the next shepherd there. His response to my urging to seek from above a Timothy (from among his flock to be mentored by him now so that later, that brother will be ready to step into the shoes of that seasoned pastor) was very positive. The Lord had indeed impressed him with that ministry as being important, and he was busy in that very task. So I promised him a follow-up article about this topic. Hope you too are blessed by what follows:

- - - -

As the Lord has caught my attention across recent years on matters that affect how His churches can make progress, He showed me several things about the early church. One of their practices was for leaders to have Timothy's which would be mentored in a personal way while the Timothy would commit to spending extra time working alongside a local pastor or traveling with a seasoned missionary.

Once you become a car owner, you will discover that even with thoughtful maintenance, cars break down mechanically, or, worse, you are involved in an accident. Now the car needs to be fixed. Now you need a mechanic who runs a well-equipped garage.

But all mechanics are not equal in terms of knowledge and skill. When you paid good money for a problem that was supposedly fixed and then drive away from the garage, if two blocks away that funny noise and that lousy symptom show up again, in frustration you figure out that you need to try to get the help of a different mechanic, a better one.

Once you do finally find a mechanic who listens to you, does a test or two on your engine, knows exactly what is your problem, orders just the right parts to replace the old worn-out ones, and charges you a fair price for his labor, you feel like that man is worth his weight in gold!

But now a question: how did that mechanic become so skilled to fix any and all car problems that need fixing? Was he born that way? No, not at all. There was a time in that man's life when the only thing he knew about a car was that it had four wheels.

So how did he go from that level of ignorance and ineptness to become a skilled mechanic with such great insight on anything that can go wrong from bumper to bumper? There is but one answer. That man got hired by a very experienced mechanic who then showed the newbie this is how you figure out the problem and then here are the answers to each problem.

The man with experience talked to the newbie, and he showed the newbie what he was doing and how. And the newbie did more than watch and listen. He assisted, and he got his hands dirty working alongside that master mechanic.

This is the source from which every society reaps new mechanics. We don't just hand the up and coming crop of garage owners and operators a pile of books to read on the internal combustion engine, and another book on all the gears of the transmission, and another book on the braking system, and another book on the muffler and exhaust system, and another book about the frame and suspension system, and another book that is all about tires.

In all occupations, we usually grasp how important it is to mentor someone into a level of good knowledge and skillful expertise. Welders must show newbies how to weld all kinds of metals. Surgeons must show their interns the way to pick up a sharp scalpel and slice open a human body with the intent to bring relief and healing instead of just endangering the sick person more. If you don't have a knowledgeable electrician to show you how to fix electrical problems safely, then I prophesy that you will get the shock of your life as you tinker with outlets where 220 volts are flowing through!

So why is it that the churches of today have followed a different course in getting our next batch of leaders prepared for their ministries? A young man or woman senses that they have just been called into ministry by the Lord. What do we do next? We send them out of the local church to some kind of external training facility called Bible schools or seminaries or something else. What happens there? Over the next two, three, or four years, those students listen to lectures, study Greek and Hebrew, buy and read *lots* of books, and then prove they can get passing grades on papers they write and tests they take.

But what is missing from this scenario? No one is *showing* them how to walk out their future ministries in shepherding or church planting or evangelism or in cross-cultural missions.

So what is it that we see produced by our fine centers of theological training? We only produce scholars.

Let me testify. When I and my peers finished up first our college undergraduate degrees and then a seminary program resulting in degrees at the master level, we were then ordained by our denominations. Then we each one headed off into our first ever full-time ministries.

Do you know what happened next? Failure. Abject failure. And with that came a truckload of frustration, not just for us newbie graduates but for those saints and sinners to whom we were trying to serve in those towns and flocks.

We figured out real quick that we really had no idea what we were doing, except one thing was sure. We surely knew how to do things the wrong way. We knew how to use those big words and theological terms they taught us in seminary, and as we talked like our professors from our pulpits, the only thing the sheep could say was, “Huh? What in the world is he talking about?” Yes, we had become mini-scholars, but not yet become compassionate shepherds.

But somehow, across those early years, if we persevered and didn’t quit our callings (which indeed some did quit), then by the grace of the Good Shepherd, He redeemed our many mistakes, and we managed to make progress toward becoming real servants of the Lord.

I recall when I lived next door to a hotel in Penang. My youngest child Jeremy would go with me to use their pool when he was six years old. Jeremy would stay in the shallow end, while I was swimming laps up and down the length of the pool.

One day, Jeremy told me, “Daddy, I want to swim a lap, too.” Well, I knew he had had only a bit of swim training so far, so I wasn’t sure he was ready for this particular challenge. But I didn’t want to discourage him either.

So I climbed out of the water so I could keep an eagle eye upon my son while walking down the side of the pool as Jeremy began his version of *swimming*. Oh my, it was not a pretty sight.

That boy launched out from the shallow end with arms and legs just flailing away. Instead of smooth arm strokes coordinated with fluid foot kicking, he made painfully slow progress as he struggled to reach the other end of the pool where it was deep. Frankly I witnessed more splashing than actual swimming.

Finally, he reached the far end and hung onto the side while gasping to catch his breath. I squatted down beside him and said, "Son, you found a way to drown yourself across the pool instead of swim across." And I think he agreed with that assessment.

That's what happens to most graduates from our scholarly theological institutes. We head back into churches to begin our ministries, but in fact what follows next isn't very pretty. We too are drowning our way across the pool.

So when I now teach and counsel the crop of middle-aged servants of the Lord and I ask them, "Who here is your Timothy?" once they realize what this concept means, they are hesitant to agree to mentor a younger saint who has just been called into ministry. Why so? Because they sense their inadequacy **to take the place of an entire seminary program all alone**.

So here is how I try to relieve their anxiety. I ask a series of rather simple questions (which all have the same simple answer). Here they are, and I pause for their answer before going on to the next one:

Do you know Psalm 23?

Do you like it?

Can you quote the first line of it? (Sure, who hasn't learned to say, "The Lord is my Shepherd?")

Is that line true for you, is Jesus really your shepherd?

If I now have four yes answers; I then ask,

"So if Jesus is your shepherd, then that makes you a… what?"

Hmm… do you see where this is going? The Scriptures do not liken believers to critters like high flying eagles not like ferocious tigers nor like bold roosters. We are called His sheep. And sheep are not God's brightest and fastest creatures. Sheep are sort of dim witted frankly.

While I served in Suriname, my church planting friend and I were in a cross-country car trip from the capital to their #2 city of Nickerie. So we used a charter taxi. It's a coastal road with the Caribbean Sea often in view. The terrain is flat, no hills.

At one point, we could all see up ahead that there was a long curve in the road. From a half mile away, we saw a small flock of sheep crossing the road we were on. Well, almost all of them crossed promptly.

But one little lamb only went part way, and then he saw our taxi coming. That must have been very interesting to this little guy, because he stopped walking right in our lane and just stared at this unusual sight of a taxi bearing down upon him. That lamb apparently sensed no danger and just stood there in the highway.

Thankfully our driver noticed this from afar, and he took his foot off the gas pedal. We kept slowing down and getting closer to the lamb, but he wouldn't budge from that spot. We finally came to a full stop with the bumper only a meter from the lamb's nose. Then his curiosity must have been satisfied because he then bleated at us and turned to go catch up to the flock. Talk about dumb!

Sure, all of us feel inadequate to become a one-man seminary education for another person. How many of us who did actually study two years of Greek and 2,000 years of church history and read many books that were published by great scholars and theologians, and how many of us actually remember all of that stuff? In all honesty, we don't.

I have adapted a riddle for my own use.

So I then ask pastors, “Could you go into a library and make a stack of books as high as you are tall, then take off your shoes, and jump over them?” They usually shake their heads to say no, they cannot do that.

Then I kick off my shoes and ask, “You mean you cannot jump over your own shoes?!” as I proceed to easily hop across my shoes.

To mentor someone does not mean to produce a new scholar but rather a new shepherd. “So pastor, could you see yourself capable to train a Timothy to become just a bit brighter than a flock of not-so-bright sheep?” Now they begin to realize that the bar is really not set so high. The high bar was set by the seminaries, not by our Lord.

A few years ago, I taught a three-night leadership seminar on Wisdom from Above in Pune, India. We had a good group of leaders, pastors, and church planters. Then at the conclusion of the three hours I taught on the last night, a young pastor in his thirties who had attended every session wanted to accompany me as I walked the half mile or so back to my lodging. He related his life story and testimony.

When he was very young, his parents both died. So he was raised in an orphanage run by Christians ‘til he was 18. During those growing up years, he gave his heart to Jesus. Then as a young man, he heard God’s call to become a full-time servant. So he attended a Bible school for three years.

Since he graduated, the Lord moved him to Pune to pioneer a new church in town.

When word was circulating that a leadership seminar was soon to happen there and that a brother Douglas from America would teach on Wisdom from Above (which includes this topic of mentoring Timothy's like the early church did), this young pastor confessed to me his skepticism about reaping anything new from that event before I arrived. After all, he had studied hard for three years in Bible school. He made good grades. He still retained much in his head from all those lectures.

But then he showed up on the first night. When you are the speaker, those who are the keen listeners really catch your eye. This young man was certainly so eager to soak up everything, hardly blinking an eye, eagerly writing down many notes.

So now when the seminar was finished, he told me his story, and he added, "Brother Douglas, I never knew your name before, you aren't famous, and I didn't expect to receive much that would be new to me. But now I must tell you, everything you taught us about across the nine hours of sessions, **I never heard any of this stuff during three years of Bible school studies!**"

Let me conclude with a scenario and a question. Do you think that that young pastor who never knew his earthly father yet he came to Jesus who is now his Lord, Jesus could lead him to marry a fine Christian young lady and then together be blessed with the fruit of the womb, and he could go on **to become a godly father for his own children**? Surely the answer is yes, that is very possible, even though he never knew his earthly father.

So too can pastors, leaders, and missionaries today who never were personally mentored in their youth by more experienced servants; they can still rise up and do for someone else what others earlier failed to do for you. You can do this.

And I believe this must be restored to all ministries today if we want to see the kind of effectiveness and fruitfulness that was evident in the days of the early church. The latter days of God's house will outshine the glory of the early days, so prophesies the prophet Haggai (Hag. 2:9). "Yes, Lord, make it happen!"

- - - -

How Important Is Local Church?

After reading the last message titled "Starting and Finishing," a brother in Texas sent me the following story which his wife had experienced:

- - - -

"At one time, my wife worked with an organization that taught kids how to witness to other kids. Then she stopped working with them and continues to not work with them because of no follow-up to help the new babies in Christ get linked in to local churches."

What follows is how this conversation continues. Hope you too are blessed:

- - - -

When we do not know or understand the importance of local church for the follow-up and discipleship of new believers, then I say simply that such servants who justify the activity of personal evangelism alone are not prepared for success.

Successful soul winning one by one is not just about an individual inner transformation from dead to alive, from non-Christian to real Christian, but also it is a change from sinful isolation from one another into a unity with… whom? With the newly acquired "family" of God. Proper understanding of what has transpired when someone repents and turns to Jesus as Lord is that he or she has just become adopted into God's family. Thus you get more than personal and private salvation. You become one of the brethren, a plural word, and you now have many brothers and sisters in Christ Jesus.

You also become a body part within the body of Jesus, with Jesus as the Head. (I now prefer the term *body part* instead of the usual word *member*. Why? Because the secular definition for *member* has usurped the Biblical use of that word, as in, if you are a member of a certain church, then it means your name is on a membership list at that church. You are part of that club, except the church is not a club.) Yet if someone who seemingly comes to Jesus in a genuine way but then is not taught of the importance of a local body of Christ to be an active part of is then likened unto a severed finger.

When I teach on this, often I take out my pocket knife and open the main blade. Then I pretend to deliberately chop off a finger and then lay it upon the pulpit. Then I spin out the following story:

Someone comes into the sanctuary and finds this gruesome sight, a bloody finger on the pulpit. So the police are called. When they arrive, the finger gets taken to the station. Why? Because every finger has a unique fingerprint. They run that print through their computer system to find out whose it is. Ta da! The answer pops out that this severed finger belongs to one Douglas Montague. Yep, they are correct, that is my finger.

But is that finger receiving a fresh flow of oxygenated blood? Nope, not while severed it isn't. But can that finger now receive instructions from the brain about touching something, or grasping, or flexing? Nope, not while severed.

This is why one body part separated and alone cannot usually prosper in the Lord. That is the position of the one who supposedly was brought to Jesus but was not properly discipled to learn of the importance of being in (and active in) a local church. Such folks are not prepared for success in the Lord, especially if this condition is self-imposed.

Sure, if I get forcefully locked away in solitary confinement, Jesus will still be with me, just as He proved that He could keep His servant Richard Wurmbrand sane while the communists locked him up that way for three years in Romania. The Lord can still be sufficient for us whenever we must be alone as He was for His servant John on the uninhabited isle of Patmos. But men like these two did not experience such isolation because it was self-imposed. The norm for the vast majority of believers is that we have enough freedom to access and attend the gatherings of saints who come together for worship and learning more of His Word.

Just because the local churches are imperfect and have various problems does not mean that local churches have no value and should be ignored or abandoned. Jesus still loves His imperfect bride. And He is still working on her by the washing of the water of His Word (Eph. 5:25–27). Jesus is still speaking to His churches as He did to seven of them via John's last letter with words both of encouragement and words of correction. He will not turn His back on His bride, and neither should we.

- - - -

An Appeal to My American Brethren

I am praying for my homeland often. I learned an expression from my Indonesian brethren when they pray aloud, and I am listening to how they make their appeals to the Lord. One in particular has caught my attention, which goes like this…

"O Tuhan, campurkanlah tanganMu di dalam perkara ini."

Translation: Oh Lord, mix Your hand in this matter.

Our nation has a godly heritage, led by men most of whom were genuine followers of Jesus and avid students of the Scriptures. They searched His Word to find principles to guide them how to put together a nation that Heaven would be pleased to bless if that nation would indeed believe in those things and walk them out.

So I know that anything that our Lord does and any nation that our Lord blesses will then immediately become the next target for our hate-filled enemy, ol' slewfoot himself. He never rests from his cruel intentions to sow as much corruption into America as his wicked heart can conjure up.

I have watched videos posted by Americans who in these recent times have signed off their pessimistic messages of gloom and doom with declarations that the situation for America is now hopeless, and thus they themselves are "getting out" while they feel that that option is still viable. I want to ask such folks a couple of things, such as, "And to where do you propose to go in this world where you think that those nations have not also experienced demonic corruption?" as well as to ask, "Do you not know that our God calls Himself the God of Hope?"

Our hope is not found in running away from the attacks of our enemy, but in running toward our God of all hope. He can turn things around in an instant. He has done it before.

Remember how powerful that evil prime minister was named Haman in Persia, and in the space of twenty-four hours, the Lord didn't just depose Haman. Haman and all of his familial allies were hung, and replacing him immediately was the humble and godly Mordecai, the Jew.

If American believers wherever they dwell, inside American states or territories, or outside, will just humble ourselves and urgently seek His face, His presence, His mighty hand to be mixed into what is going on with those who plot and plan against the founding principles upon which our homeland rests, then surely we too shall witness what our God of hope can do for our nation. American believers do *not* have to wait 'til November to see something good happen for our country. Why set our hopes upon the political process and the political calendar? Our God can mix His mighty hand into the affairs of men at any time, any day, and any season.

"In Jesus name, Lord, bring us again to Your throne of grace that we may again receive of your mercy and obtain sufficient grace for these times of great need, to the glory of King Jesus, Amen."

- - - -

Who Wrote Job?

Just got this from a pastor friend not far from the Thai border.

- - - -

Shalom Doug,

Thank you for all the articles, sharing, and testimonies. God is indeed a good God. His *goodness* is over you and family. I have come down with a fever, flu, and cough but not Covid; I am just a bit weak though. Trust all is well with you.

Your student has a question here:

Who is the author of the book of Job? I am wondering who recorded the detailed conversation between Job and his three friends.

Thank you, my brother.

- - - -

So here was my reply to my friend and fellow servant over here in Southeast Asia. Hope you too are blessed:

- - - -

I have stepped past the torn curtain once again, into the presence of the Father who always wants to see the name of His Son to be more and more glorified (for Jesus is worthy), and I have reminded the Most High what He has proclaimed that there is healing power within those terrible painful stripes that Jesus endured, healing for you to be raised up *now* with renewed strength and vigor and thus to give you a fresh word of testimony in your ongoing ministry to folks both near and far away so that I expect His hand to be mixed in the affair of your health and the uplifting of your soul to magnify our Lord more and more.

As to the matter of who sat down and composed the content of the book of Job, look up again the following verses, found at Job 19:23–29. In short, the most likely human author of this amazing story which truly happened and is not a fictional parable is the man Job himself. Your question in this matter is not just a scholarly detail to track down. For in this answer that Job is the author, it reveals something much deeper and more marvelous than just chasing down an obscure detail.

Look at how the story is presented to us. Chapters 1 and 2 tell us clearly that Satan himself is very involved and primarily the source of all of Job and Mrs. Job's (since we don't know her name… yet) suffering and loss.

But when you look at all the back and forth between Job and his three *friends* which are in chapters 3–31, the four of them keep talking about Job's situation with a presumption that God Almighty is the cause of all of Job's great trial. Only once does Job himself bring up the possibility that if it is not the Lord, then who could it be? See Job 9:24c.

Then you get the six chapters of the younger man, Elihu, who had also shown up when the three older friends arrived, and apparently he sat quietly during all the lengthy debate back and forth between the three who keep trying to persuade Job that this has happened because Job must have sin or sins in his life of which Job needs to repent, and Job repeatedly declaring, "I don't know of any sins in my life to acknowledge as to why God is afflicting me now." But the six chapters of Elihu's response to Job do *not* elicit a rebuke in chapter 42 from the Lord.

So when we read those six chapters, we would do well to notice a qualitative difference in Elihu's assessment and counsel with that of the older three friends of Job. Elihu's message is to bring attention again and again to how high the Lord is, that He is holy, that He will not perform injustice, and that His thoughts and ways are above ours, so Job needs to stop accusing the Lord of not doing right by him.

Now here's the real kicker in relation to your original question. Now you reach the four chapters (38–41) of God Almighty's response and rebuke to Job himself. And what do you and I find strangely missing in those four chapters? Not once does the Lord straighten out Job's understanding about who is responsible for his suffering, that is, "It ain't Me, Job, it is the devil!" No. Instead we find four chapters of rhetorical questions put before Job, questions whose answers are indeed obviously implied from the question itself, such as, "Where were you, Job, when I laid the foundation of the earth?" (Job 38:4). The rebuke of the Lord to Job is to get Job to humble himself **to turn away from his anger**.

Whenever any of us justify our overflowing anger with anyone, including anger toward the Lord, we do so because we believe we know enough to justify our anger. Review again how the Lord dealt with Jonah in chapter 4. Twice the Lord asks Jonah, "Do you have **good reason** to be angry?" (Jon. 4:4, 9).

But the seventy plus questions that the Lord puts to Job is to first bring him back to the reality of who Job is. Job is a little man with a very limited understanding about all of God's creation (Job 40:3–5 and 42:3b, c).

So once Job repents of all of his accusations against the Lord and then obeys the Lord in relation to his three friends who wrongly accused Job of sin, then we see the Lord turn everything around for him in the remainder of chapter 42.

But wait! That work of the Lord to turn things around for Job **must also include giving Job more revelation as to what**

happened to him and why, which is what we call the content of chapters 1 and 2, all about Satan and his wager with Lord.

So the human author of that part of our Bible is the man Job himself. But the real Author is none other than the Lord Himself, for without the Lord's gracious revealing of what transpired in chapters 1 and 2, then Job's story would be very very incomplete.

- - - -

The All-Knowing One

An Oklahoma friend posted an item that I appreciated, and then it prompted one of my testimonies along these same lines. Hope you too are blessed by both offerings:

- - - -

"Satan is a master theologian. He's talked to God, interacted with God, believes in God's existence, and knows more about God's attributes and abilities than most, and yet Satan doesn't love God. Knowledge about God does not equal faith in God."

- - - -

To that, I replied with the following:

Yes, well said. And may I add, the Lord had to correct my thinking about my works and my warfare against Satan.

Back in my Chess playing youth, that game had become a "god" in my life. It consumed far too much of my time in my devotion to get ahead among the world of chess players who took that game so seriously. So after coming to Jesus as Lord, I pretty much turned away from staring at that board of sixty four squares and put much more time into searching the Scriptures.

But in my walk with Jesus, for a while, an image taken from the world of chess occupied my thoughts. Now that I was saved, I knew He had works for me to fulfill and that I had an enemy to deal with in warfare.

Chess is like a war played out between two opponents. So for a time, I thought I was in charge of the white pieces, and my opponent was none other than Satan himself who controlled the black pieces. Once you get passed the second move of the game, the number of possibilities on how to continue are almost endless. That's why chess is not for the faint of heart nor weak of mind. You must develop chess vision to be able to see ahead to determine if a certain course of play will work to your advantage or instead will weaken your own position overall.

That kind of burden to believe that it is my job to outwit and outthink the devil in order to win the game for the Lord is just too much for me or for anyone. So the Lord got through to me eventually that my concept needed correcting.

He said, "Son, you are not a player at the chess board with a task to beat the devil." Surprised, I responded, "Oh? Well if that's the case, then who am I in this whole matter of my warfare against Your enemy and mine?" He then said, "You're not a player, you are a piece." So then I asked, "Well, if I am not running the white pieces, then who is?" He smiled and said, "That's My job!"

What a tremendous shift in concept! What relief that has brought to my mind and heart. I don't have to become smart enough to finally outwit the devil during my years upon the earth. I can relax knowing that I am but one piece on the chessboard called planet earth.

Whenever He wants, He can move me forward. When He wants me to attack, He will put me in that position. When He wants me to block or to be blocked, He again arranges all of that. If He wants me as a lowly pawn to successfully navigate all the way across the board to the eighth rank and then be promoted into a more valuable piece, He knows how to make that happen. And if in His goal to get the victory, He decides it is time to sacrifice a piece, even myself, then He can be trusted to have thoughts higher than my thoughts.

Just think how doomed the enemy is to lose that game facing an Opponent who knows all things, who can read the thoughts of your mind, and who understands every wicked intent of your heart as to why you make each move on the board. The devil has no hope for victory as he sits across the board from the All-Knowing One.

\- - - -

Who Is Innocent?

After a brother in Texas sent me his thoughtful reply to the article called "Who Wrote Job," the following bubbled up inside me. The story of Job brings up the whole topic of innocence. Many times, after something bad happens to us, we want to declare that we didn't deserve that, that we are innocent victims perpetrated by some evil villain figure. So consider the following from what His Word says about who it is that is truly innocent:

- - - -

You know, this concept that so many hold on to, including among the brethren at times, is that some people are good people, they are *innocent*. Therefore they do not deserve the bad things that come their way to afflict them.

But if you are ready to be blown away in regard to that idea, go read a verse that came off the page at me one time as I was going through the mostly neglected or ignored book called Lamentations. I mean, with a sad name like that, who can blame the saints or His servants for avoiding such a downer of a book in our Bibles.

Here it is…

"Why should any living man, or any mortal, offer complaint in view of his sins?" (Lamentations 3:39)

Whenever we want to declare, "I don't deserve this (whatever) happening to me," just stop and review what it is that you and I do actually deserve.

"The wages of sin is death… " (Rom. 6:23a)

So, do I have sin in my life? Oh, yes. So, what do I deserve? Death, eternal separation from the Holy God who made me, unending suffering, and pain away from His glorious presence. That's what I deserve. *But,* **thanks to Jesus, I won't get what I deserve! Hallelujah!**

Instead I get what I definitely don't deserve, which is salvation, redemption, sanctification, and eventually even glorification, all by His grace, His mercy, His faithfulness, and His compassion. I get to have a real friendship with my Lord now, which is a walk by faith, and that my friendship with Him will continue forever once I cross over and then walk with Him by sight.

And I don't deserve any of those marvelous things. So we need to get off this jag of allowing ourselves to think or believe that there is anyone besides Jesus who doesn't deserve bad things when those things hit us out of left field.

Only Jesus was and is totally innocent. No one else. Even the judge, Pontius Pilate, said three times about Jesus, "I find no guilt in Him." Jesus did *not* deserve the following:

- Betrayal by His treasurer
- Abandonment by His disciples
- Denial three times by Peter
- Flogging with a cat o' nine tails
- A crown of ironlike thorns beaten down into His scalp
- Being punched out repeatedly while surrounded by a bunch of pissed off Roman soldiers
- Carrying His cross up a hill while under complete exhaustion
- Stripped naked just before they crucified Him
- Getting His hands and feet nailed with spikes into the wood of the Cross
- The taunts and mockery from the priests as He hung upon the Cross
- The offer of soured wine held up to His lips after He said, "I thirst"
- Getting stabbed in His side with a spear
- And finally giving up His spirit to breathe His last time before embracing death

Did I leave anything out? Jesus didn't deserve any of that nor all of that.

But you and I and all the sinners of this world do indeed deserve those things which were poured out upon Him. If we review these truths yet can refrain from turning to Him with another “Thank you, Lord Jesus, for taking my place,” then we certainly must have awfully calloused hearts.

- - - -

To Encourage a Newbie to the Field

Last October, while Ruth and I attended a Missions Conference in Ohio, we met a young man who was on the cusp of entering the Lord's service abroad in the island of Mindanao. Having also served four times in that region a few years ago, I have some familiarity with what he has begun to cope with since his arrival there two months ago.

He just contacted me a few days ago, asking how long it took to get a working knowledge of a second language. So I sent him a copy of the testimony article that I composed earlier this summer titled "To Acquire a Second Tongue." But not satisfied with that, I also wanted to invest more into this newbie to cross-cultural work.

So the following will let you listen in on how I am seeking to counsel and encourage him as his first main task is to break into their local language. Oftentimes, that goal seems overwhelming. But with the Lord's help, it can be accomplished because Jesus Himself became flesh and dwelt among us, using the local lingo in all of His earthly ministry.

I wrongly assumed he was now tackling Cebuano, but later he informed me that he's dealing with Maguindanaon, a tongue I had not yet heard of. So just substitute that long word for every time you see me refer to Cebuano.

- - - -

One tip: don't become impatient with your progress. Something is happening every day that you are among that people group. You are hopefully listening to them. Listening is the foundation for all language acquisition.

Americans have a positive reputation in this world about some things. But listening isn't one of them.

You need to pay attention to **how the locals express things**. Then you imitate them.

Your daily encounters with locals will constantly bring up situations in which you are trying to cope… and yet, for lack of certain vocabulary, you will have one temporary failure after another. This is normal. Let these little frustrations become your incentive to go get a few more words of vocabulary that will help you function better the next time.

Keep in mind who you are and who you are not. Are you a big horsey adult? Yes, but only in English. In Cebuano, **you**

are an infant. And being at such an immature and inexperienced level in that lingo, your local friends are not always being helpful (even though they seem eager to help you learn their language) **when they try to dump upon you too much too soon**.

One of the best ways you can make progress is by those occasions when you can be near very young children as they interact with the adults around them. Why? Because you are in the same boat with those youngins.

Adults know that you cannot tell a toddler a long involved sentence and then expect compliance nor understanding. We talk to them in one-word or two-word statements. No. Stop. Cannot. Come here. Let's go. Sit down. Please sit.

When you ask a local friend, "What's the word for...?," guess what happens. First, they tell you a word, and then they want to refine it and tell you that at certain times or conditions, that's the wrong word, so instead you should say (blank), and then they blather on about other nuances, and your heart is sinking through the floor with discouragement. It's called *information overload*. And they do this to the foreigner quite innocently because their eyes and their minds tell them that you are a tall fully grown adult. Yes, you are, but not in their local tongue, not yet.

So you must actually take charge in your relationships with the other adults around you so that you guide them on how to help you make progress in their tongue. Not even a hired language tutor can take charge of your progress.

If you're familiar with the LAMP program (Language Acquisition Made Practical), then you can follow their acrostic for making some progress every day in that language. It is G-L-U-E-E:

- Get what you need.
- Learn what you got.
- Use what you learn.
- Evaluate how it went.
- Envision what you need next.

Once you get an agreement from a local to be your language helper, not your tutor, then you follow the steps of GLUEE.

Day one. You need five things.

Ask your helper how you can do the following:

1. Properly greet folks when you meet them. Write it down. Record your helper saying those things.

2. Tell folks that you are learning Cebuano. Again, write it down. Record your helper.

3. Express your limitation that this is all you know so far. Write. Record.

4. How can you express gratitude for them listening to you. Write. Record.

5. How to properly take your leave of them. Again, write and record.

This doesn't take half an hour. Then your helper goes away, and it's time for the L in GLUEE. Spend thirty minutes *learning* your little five-line spiel, using your written notes and listening to your recordings.

Then comes the most important letter, U for *use what you got*. You hit the streets and the shops, you walk up to total strangers, and you let 'em have it. If you have fifty brief encounters that day, you're doing well. This is the most time-consuming step.

Before the return of your language helper the next day or every other day, you need to implement the two Es of GLUEE. Evaluate how it went. Did folks understand you? Did they smile, or did they look confused?

Then you must envision what you need next from your language helper so that when he arrives, you are prepared to Get the next thing that you need.

This is a framework which I found helpful. But not being a legalist, I also gave myself permission to be flexible. So change things up as you see fit.

But always keep in mind that the Lord has you there for building relationships, for those are the bridges across which His messages of truth, wisdom, and love can cross over to reach their hearts. And there's no better way to build those relationships than by breaking into their local lingo. So never discount the importance of making progress in acquiring their language.

- - - -

Then he told me that he is enrolled in a language school. So that prompted the following:

- - - -

I hope you have lots of time interacting with locals in their normal settings and not stay much confined to a sterile classroom setting. There is a difference between studying a language and learning a language.

I still recall the first two questions which the professor asked our class of mission candidates (seventy-five to eighty folks, all with bachelor degrees and above) back in summer of 1982."

"How many of you have ever studied any foreign language?"

Every hand went up.

"How many of you became fluent in any foreign language that you studied?"

Every hand went back down.

"Why not? Because you did exactly that. You studied a foreign language but you did not learn a foreign language."

And we concluded our chat at that point with his response of "Wow!"

- - - -

To Encourage a Newbie (Part 2)

An Indonesian friend who tutors kids in her home to help them learn English wrote back just now, asking,

"By the way, what is the difference between study and learn?"

My answer:

Study is analytical.

Learning is what happens by experience.

By the time a child is five to six years old, that kid is now fluent in their first language. Yet they never studied it so far. They learned it passively, not in a proactive studying mode.

The parents did not hand a dictionary to the child at age three to increase the child's vocabulary. The child knows how to mention objects in singular or plural but does not yet know what the word *plural* means.

The child knows and uses many nouns, verbs, adjectives, adverbs, prepositions, and interrogatives but does not actually know the meaning of those grammar terms yet.

That only happens once they start attending a formal school setting and the student begins to study his own language that he already knows how to speak and listen to.

Her reply:

Oh Ok. I see. I see.
Yes, understood.

Thanks, pastor. 🙏

- - - -

Here's another piece to the puzzle on how everyone acquires their first language.

One more tip that we garner from watching little kiddos make progress in their first language acquisition is this:

Learn a little,

Use it a lot!

...which happens to be the *opposite* of how we run language classes in school settings!

I walked into German class for the first time ever. On Monday, day 1, I was given a handout with twenty-five words that would be on the Friday quiz.

So I dutifully went home and memorized that list of words so I could spit it back out on test day to get an A+. I succeeded. But in spite of my good grades in German, if I ran into an actual German speaker, I had no more idea how to communicate with him than with the Man in the Moon! Ugh!

Little kids grab onto one or two concepts and then repeat them over and over. The toddler in the bathtub with his floating toys grabs a little man in one hand and a plastic boat in the other hand and then demonstrates that he can say and do "in the boat" followed by yanking the little man out and then says "out of the boat." Over and over with glee. Now the kid understands the two prepositions of "in" and "out." Got it!

But in formal classroom settings, we do things backward. We expect students to study a lot of things in that other language, but then we use them very little or none at all.

On day one, we expect students to start speaking in that other language when they have had little to no practice yet **in listening to that other language**. But listening to the people around you since you left the womb was the foundation for eventually starting to talk and imitate what you had been hearing.

No baby or toddler is judgmental about what they hear. They don't think that Chinese sounds strange or Spanish sounds dumb, nor do they think English is so confusing. **They don't pass judgment**. They passively listen, and what they hear is just normal to them.

So when one wishes to break into another language, you will do yourself a favor if you refrain from saying to yourself (or worse, out loud for others near you to hear), "Well that sure is stupid," or "How strange," or "Why do they say it that way?" When you make negative comments about their language, you are short-circuiting your own progress to acquire theirs.

Just learn to say, "Oh, well, that's different," without an added tone of scoffing or derision. Then you will be seen by those around you as one who values and esteems their language.

No one dislikes their first language. No one. So showing them your happy willingness to apply yourself to acquire their lingo will win you miles and miles of favor in their hearts.

- - - -

Don't Waste Your Access!

Recently, I have rather boldly gone into His presence on behalf of two friends from our college days and told the Lord that since He granted me to become a priest who has access to His throne of grace that in no uncertain terms, no wishy-washy requests on my part, that I want to make clear my godly desire to seek for a complete and glorious recovery for him after his recent surgery and for his sweet wife who does *not* need to lose her mind as predicted by her doctors but instead can be like the man in Gadara who was sitting at the feet of Jesus **in his right mind**. The Lord gives His people His Spirit who brings to us "a sound mind" (2 Tim. 1:7).

From where does this new boldness in intercessory prayer arise? I must honestly confess that in bygone years, my hesitancy to seriously request much from on high was stymied by a sort of fatalism. Oh sure, as we walk with the Lord, read our Bibles, and listen to messages at church, we all hear many admonitions to be a people of prayer.

But in my heart, I had somewhat reasoned my way into very low expectations of anything happening for others or for myself because I had boldly prayed about something. "God is going to do what God is going to do, with or without my prayers for something or against something. So why bother? Why put much effort or heart into intercession?"

Of course, the Lord knows where we are in our walk with Him. He knows where we are wrong in our thinking. It's said that stinking thinking leads to stinking theology. That's probably a pretty good observation.

So I am very grateful that the Lord has begun to open my eyes about something. As a matter of practice, I read through all of the gospel accounts once every three months. During this summer, the Lord got me to consider what happened in the Temple at the exact moment when Jesus cried out, "Father, into Your hands I commit My spirit," and then He gave up His spirit. Yes, at that moment, you hear a tremendous ripping sound, and the priests in the Temple were stunned to see… what?

According to Flavius Josephus (37–100 AD), a Jewish priest and historian, the veil that separated the holy place from the Holy of holies was 9 cm (a bit more than 3.5 inches) thick. When the first Temple was built in Solomon's days, that space for the Holy of holies measured at 20 cubits, that is, 30 feet, in length, width, and height (1 Kings 6:19, 20).

So that was one very impressive curtain indeed! I don't think I have ever laid eyes on a piece of sewn material that heavy duty.

And yet, at the moment of Jesus' death upon Calvary, the veil in the Temple was torn asunder from top to bottom, so says Matt. 27:51; Mark 15: 38; and Luke 23:45. I will come back to this matter shortly of the veil which separated the Holy place from the Holy of holies.

According to Hebrews 8:4 and 5, there are parallels between the Tabernacle on earth (whose design and layout were also used for the Temple that Solomon later built) which Moses was told to construct so that it copied the original Tabernacle which was erected by the Lord in Heaven. Hebrews 9:11 and 24 emphasizes that Jesus, after His death, then went into the Tabernacle **not made by the hands of men**. Where is that Tabernacle? In Heaven.

I still recall a humourous encounter that happened to me just after I landed in Trinidad a few years back. A certain brother was given the task by his pastor to fetch me from the airport and bring me to the pastor's home.

I cannot recall his name, but I will never forget his excitement at some news story that he had just heard. Seems that in Israel, a group of archeologists were digging somewhere and had just discovered an underground hidden chamber which led to more chambers. Commentators then speculated that maybe they would soon search through all those spaces and might finally discover where the original Tabernacle and all of its furnishings, including the Ark of the Covenant, were hidden away before Jerusalem fell into the hands of the conquering Babylonians.

So this brother asked me with great eagerness what did I think about that. I calmly replied, “Well, if they do find all that stuff and bring it out to show the world, sure, it will be interesting, but it won’t really be that important.”

Oh my! He shot me a glance which said that he thought he had been sent to go pick up a flaming heretic who just arrived to his nation. “Not important?! What do you mean?”

I asked him, “Brother, haven’t you ever read the book of Hebrews? It states clearly that what Moses made was just a copy of the original. So the Tabernacle that interests me more is not the one on earth, but the one that we believers will see one day when we enter Heaven. That’s the one Jesus entered with His own blood to put on the mercy seat and win our salvation for us.”

If you go to a famous art museum, you can see the *Mona Lisa*, mounted in a bulletproof glass case where armed guards stand nearby keeping watch on all the patrons who come to gaze upon it. Before you leave the museum, there is a gift shop where copies of that painting can be purchased for $20 apiece. If I were allowed to hold up the genuine Mona Lisa in my right han, and also hold up a copy of the Mona Lisa in my left hand, which one is worth more? The original is priceless!

Originals are always valued much much higher than mere copies of them.

In recent times, the Lord brought my attention to two particular passages in Hebrews, one at 6:19 and 20 and the other at 10:19 and 20. They both mention about the veil which was mounted at the opening to the Holy of holies. Jesus entered that holiest place in the presence of His holy Father, but to do so, Jesus had to get past the veil. But unlike how earthly high priests would pull back one side of the veil or the other side in order to enter the Holy of holies, it says that Jesus entered *through* the veil (Heb. 10:19, 20).

So what did the Father do to facilitate the entrance of His Son into the real Holy of holies in Heaven? At the conclusion of all of Jesus' pain and suffering that culminated in His giving up His spirit to embrace death, the Father ripped into two pieces the veil in Heaven because Jesus was about to come there in the Spirit bringing with Him His own precious blood to place it upon the Mercy Seat (Heb. 9:11, 12, 26).

So as the veil in Heaven was torn into two pieces to signify that the way into the Father's presence had now been opened by the event of the beaten, bloodied, and pierced body of Jesus, and then the Father wanted this event to be known on the earth as well. Thus two strong angels in position at the top two corners of the veil in the Temple in Jerusalem heard the Father command loudly, "*Now!*" And any Jewish priests in the vicinity of the Holy place were shocked to see and hear that extremely thick single veil get torn into two separate pieces so that the way into the Holy of holies was now open! The resurrected Jesus went through the torn veil, torn from top to bottom, from Heaven all the way down to the bottom of the veil on earth. The living Jesus went through His own torn flesh to bring His blood as the only sacrifice that could take away all of our sins.

Now who is it that was allowed and ordained to ever enter the Holy of holies upon the earth? Go study Leviticus 16. That whole chapter is about the single day of the year, called the Day of Atonement, when the High Priest (starting with Aaron and later one of his descendants) could enter behind the veil into the Holy of holies.

The Lord gave very specific instructions on what the high priest had to do before entering that most holy place, during, and immediately after he went out from there. He had to wear very specific clothing, right down to his underwear! He had to bring in various blood sacrifices, those being from a bull, a ram, and a goat. He had to also burn incense. He had to send out a scapegoat. He had to sprinkle blood a certain number of times and at designated objects. And so serious was the Lord in all of these demands that Moses warned Aaron that he had better get this all right "lest you die" (Lev. 16:13).

So now get back to Hebrews. At 3:1, we are told to "consider Jesus, the Apostle and High Priest of our confession." These two titles apply to Jesus sequentially, as in, first, He fulfills

His role as Apostle until His death, and then He fulfills His role as High Priest.

The word *apostle* simply means "one who has been sent." If you read the entire Gospel according to John, you cannot miss how many many times the words *send* or *sent* are found in relation to Jesus and His earthly ministry. The works of Jesus (John 5:36) and the words of Jesus (John 12:49) were all rooted in the matter that He did and said those things just as the Father *sent* Him to do and to say. And then the culmination of all the *send* passages is when the resurrected Jesus meets with His apostles and tells them, "As the Father has sent Me, even so I send you" (John 20:21).

After His last and most important work, which was to yield up His spirit and breathe His last upon the Cross, Jesus then began to fulfill the next role that the Father ordained for Him, which is to be our High Priest. But how could that be possible if Jesus wasn't descended from the lineage that traced back to Aaron? Now you need to start at Hebrews chapter 6, verse 19 and 20 and plow ahead through all of chapter 7.

This is where two High Priests are compared. Long before Aaron was ever born, there was a priest who came and blessed Abraham, and that Hebrew forefather even paid a tithe to that priest, named Melchizedek. The summary is this: Jesus isn't likened to the priesthood of Aaron. Jesus is a High Priest according to the order of Melchizedek. See also Heb. 5:6 and 10.

John and Peter both make mention that the Lord has done something wonderful for all who receive Jesus as Lord. John says that He has made us to become priests unto the Father (Rev. 1:5, 6). Peter says that we are now a royal priesthood (1 Pet. 2:9). How is that possible? Because Jesus is our High Priest who now lives inside of each heart that opens to Him!

Aaron could only access the intimate presence of the Lord once a year. But our priesthood is so much better! Through the torn curtain which was accomplished by Jesus at Calvary, the way has been opened for each believer in Him to "boldly come to His throne of grace that we may receive mercy and may find grace in time of need" (Heb. 4:16).

For over forty years, since I first learned of the importance of the verse at John 14:6, where Jesus said, "I am the way, the truth, and the life; no one comes to the Father but *through* Me," I have almost exclusively made use of this clear statement in personal evangelism. I have encouraged many saints to memorize this verse, which, thus far, I can now quote in four languages so that if they don't hear anything else from me besides this one truth, I know that the kernel of the Gospel has been sown into their hearts.

But now, I am appreciating a different facet of this precious diamond. That verse isn't just helpful to win souls. When Jesus says that no one comes to the Father except *through* Him, I now see something that I hadn't recognized before.

The Father is waiting for me in the Holy of holies. He has clothed me in the priestly garb of the righteousness of His Son Jesus. He has already opened the way for me to easily enter His presence at any time through the torn veil which was done by the suffering and cruel death of His Son.

So why should I waste this precious gift of access? Why should I doubt that when I come into His presence with the requests and the intercession for the saints or for the sinners that I won't be heard or that Heavenly answers won't be forthcoming? My word! Why has it taken so long to come into this marvelous revelation? One thing is for sure. The Lord knows me better than I know myself.

He knew what the priest Zacharias needed in his senior years. More than needing a baby, he needed relief from his bitterness against the Lord for what seemed like long unanswered prayer as to why he and Elizabeth were childless. Thus, the Lord arranged it so that the lot fell to Zacharias to go into the Temple to burn incense, and while there, that's where the condition of his own jaded heart was made manifest to himself. Before you reach the end of Luke chapter 1, now we see a priest full of joy and praise for His God.

So I too now thank the Lord for removing my fatalistic views that were sabotaging my readiness to intercede for whomever, wherever, and whenever. The veil has been torn into two pieces, from top to bottom. Intimacy with the Father is now available twenty-four hours a day. All because of what our Jesus was willing to go through so that you and I can also go through! Hallelujah to You again, oh Lord Jesus!

\- - - -

Jesus Will Return for—Whom?

In recent years, the Lord has opened doors for me over in Borneo. Now with travel somewhat restored in this region, I have been corresponding with some of my contacts over there, seeking for more chances to invest myself in their training centers and their church planting efforts.

But lo and behold, one such brother had some sobering news to relate. His oversight of such an informal place to train saints from the villages has now become officially affiliated with a certain denomination since 2020. So the status for me to go and co-labor with them there is now more like a red light than a green light. Until if or when I meet with approval by their formal apparatus, my former invitations are now MIA, missing in action. Hmm….

So here is how I have tried to caution my fellow laborer over there who at the moment has had to wave me off. Here's another peek into my world of how to interact with indigenous leadership. Hope you are edified, blessed, and forewarned:

- - - -

For my way of functioning in a more informal way, I could wish that you were still flowing in the previous way. A one-line joke my father (who was a full-time pastor for thirty-eight years) would quote from time to time (after a rather frustrating church business meeting) was this:

For God so loved the world that He did *not* send a committee!

Lawyers and denominational leaders are known for one word they use over and over:

No!

But once you and I had met for the first time, you sensed the Lord telling you, "This man is ok." So you opened the door for me to come bless and edify those who came from the villages to your training center with sound and helpful teaching from His Word.

Now if I am allowed to come serve among those flocks or schools, first I must jump through their hoops?

My question is this: why don't headquarters trust that proven men like you have the ability to exercise discernment about those who volunteer to come and enrich those young disciples in the wisdom of His Word but instead this kind of restriction that only a certain few at the top know how to do so means that they don't care that this demand actually insults you and denies that you have sufficient maturity in Him to make those kinds of decisions?

I am truly sorry that this is how they are treating you, my brother. Shameful, quite shameful, and so unnecessary.

May the Lord still guide you how to move forward in spite of these attempts to cripple the progress of your ministry and outreach.

Am quite sure there is more to your story than I know now, but the revealing of that story is up to you if you care to share it.

What I wonder is summed up in Paul's question to the churches in Galatia when he asked them, "You were running well; who hindered you from obeying the truth?" (Gal. 5:7).

To my perspective (which I know is much less informed than yours), it seemed to me that your training center was functioning quite nicely without any official attachment to a denomination. So it begs the question, what kind of advantage now adheres to your center because of coming under their auspices?

As you have heard me teach in the classroom as well as shared across our plates of lovely chicken and rice at your local eateries, the Lord has brought my attention over these recent years to an appreciation for how the early church functioned. With so much to admire about the churches and their ministries, including how they imitated the ways of Jesus to **mentor the next crop of church planters, pastors, and missionaries in a very personal way**, I have realized that they were three things. They were simple, and fertile, and reproductive.

But after the second century concluded, churches everywhere seem to be inexorably drawn to become the opposite. Instead of being simple, now denominations practically boast in their complexity. Instead of being concerned with growth toward becoming mature in the Lord through a richness in His Word, denominational leaders seem more concerned with its leadership becoming more scholarly via academia and their degrees and titles that they hand out. Instead of churches becoming mother churches who birth daughter churches continuously, denominational leaders become far too occupied with how local flocks should show headquarters their loyalty even while those local churches are languishing and barely surviving, let alone reproducing themselves.

I myself was raised in formal Christendom. In history almost 200 years ago, the movements that birthed the founding of lively New Testament style flocks (which eventually became my original denomination) were indeed simple, fertile, and reproductive. But sadly, I must honestly report that my kind of church in which I was raised is now in fact one of the fastest dying mainline denominations in all of America.

This is my concern. A few years ago, while I was serving in Sarawak, one such pastor told me that a recent decision came down from headquarters saying that there would no longer be any concern nor effort expended to try and plant more churches. That pastor was in shock. I fully sympathized with his consternation.

You know that 500 years ago, that period of church history is called the "Reformation." Yesterday I decided to watch once again on YouTube the 1953 film simply called *Martin Luther*. Today I am watching another one, called *John Hus* who preceded *Martin Luther* by about a hundred years.

But I have often thought that it is a misnomer to call 1517 the start of the Reformation. Why? Because to be more accurate would mean we should call it "The Attempted Reformation," for it was indeed Martin Luther's fervent desire to bring about reforms **for the entire Catholic system of belief and practice**. If he and other so-called reformers had truly succeeded, then there would no longer be any Catholicism, which is still around and still full of man-made doctrines and man-made traditions and man-made rituals.

And now across my own lifetime, I have known personally three men who became modern-day reformers who sincerely tried for decades to bring about a renewal movement of my denomination, only to eventually realize that headquarters did *not* appreciate any of their efforts to get back on track with sound Bible teaching, nor return to a simpler form of local church, nor re-engage with frontline missions in this world. Reformation? What exactly got reformed? Instead, we keep learning what Jesus taught is indeed true, which is that new wine can only be stored in new wineskins, not old ones. So those three leaders have finally realized it was time to quit beating a dead horse, and they reluctantly established a new fellowship of churches who are like minded in belief and practice.

So may the Lord give you His wisdom on how to proceed from here. As you do so, please keep in mind that Jesus is not coming back for a well-oiled, highly organized business. He is coming back for a bride.

- - - -

The Cure for Dry and Stagnant Churches

After the brother in Borneo got the last message called "Jesus Will Return for—Whom?", he was quite pleased and then replied with more information about those churches, plus added some questions. Hope you are blessed to keep following this chat:

- - - -

Thanks so much for the great lessons from your *history lesson*, Big Bro in the Lord. Our church is not quite like any of the mainline denominations; it's uniquely indigenous. Thanks to the missionaries who pioneered these flocks for their wisdom in raising and establishing this as an indigenous church. Up till about the early 2000s, it was acknowledged as the fastest-growing church in Malaysia.

For a time, it kind of stalled. Today, sadly speaking, we are experiencing it starting to go inexorably in the unproductive way, as you explained.

With your world-wide missionary experiences and gained wisdom, what would you see for us as a remedy for stagnant and unproductive churches or combating spiritual dryness? And by the way, I love the last sentence of your concerned sharing, "He is coming back for a bride."

- - - -

To combat spiritual dryness, the first thing that comes to mind is that one needs to double-check one's faith in the resurrected Jesus. Yes, if you ask most anyone who claims to be a Christian a doctrinal question of "Is Jesus dead or alive?", they will give you the correct doctrinal answer: "Yes, Jesus is alive" because technically that's what the term *resurrection* means.

But I am not talking about doctrinal correctness. I am talking about me or you or anyone who says "Jesus is Lord." Do we actually have an interactive friendship with Him that is refreshed on a day-by-day basis? If that isn't happening, then that is the source of all dryness and stagnation, in my humble opinion.

Last year around this time, Ruth and I were still making rounds inside the United States. We spent one weekend visiting a couple who now lived in Arkansas, but we had first known them in their Central Texas home for many years. While spending those nights there, we attended their new church home on Sunday and heard their pastor's message.

On Monday, before we hit the highway to our next destination of Shreveport, Louisiana, we had lunch with that couple plus their pastor joined us. While waiting for our order to be brought, I mentioned to that pastor how the Lord had impressed upon me during my college years that the five words of Jesus found in John 10 had really become foundational in my life and ministry ever since, which words are, "My sheep hear My voice."

That pastor who was at least middle aged or a bit above then told me soberly that in his entire life, he felt like he had only *heard* something personal from Jesus on two occasions, and he was uncomfortable with the idea that anyone should think that *hearing* from Jesus would be a regular thing to happen.

That man would be considered a well-educated seminary graduate from a theologically conservative school and thus very evangelical, yet he justifies having a "personal relationship with Jesus" which in fact is sounding like it's very dry and impersonal.

What is wrong with this picture?

He's got the doctrine correct. Jesus is resurrected from the dead. But he doesn't really expect to have a lively friendship with the living Jesus.

Hebrews 4:12 is rather famous: "The Word of God is living and active…."

Hold on. Who is "the Word of God"? According to John 1:14, the Word became flesh and dwelt among us. Oh! That would be Jesus then.

So we could rewrite Heb. 4:12 like this:

"Jesus is living and active…"

So time is divided into three segments; that of past, and present, and future. But for my purpose, I will change up the order.

Ask any Christian, "What did Jesus do or say in the past?" and they will usually be able to tell you quite a few things about Jesus in the past, about 2,000 years ago. Fine.

Then ask, "What will Jesus do in the future?" and some saints are not very well versed in Bible prophecies that haven't been fulfilled just yet. But even still they know He will come back one day and rule the earth from Jerusalem for a thousand years. Fine again.

But now here's where the saints get really stumped. Then ask, "And what is Jesus doing today?" Here's where we get some long uncomfortable silences, sprinkled with a few, "Uhh… well… hmm… I… I am not sure."

Thus many of the saints agree that we had a very active Jesus in the past, and when He returns to earth, He will again be very active ruling the world. But in between that long-ago ministry and that future ruling of the nations, we seem to have a very passive Jesus.

But Heb. 4:12 doesn't leave room for a passive, uninvolved, unconcerned, inactive, sleepy, or vacationing Jesus off to the other side of the universe. He is the living *and active One*.

But we, His people, act at times as if all action just depends upon us for whatever acts that we think need to happen. Methinks this is something that needs both our attention and our humble repentance.

I am glad you enjoyed the concluding statement in the last missive which declared, "He is coming back for a bride." But before He comes for her, what does His Word say He is doing in relation to His bride to get her ready for His return? Jesus is "washing her with the water of His Word" (Eph. 5:26, 27). He is sanctifying her and making her holy. That doesn't sound like a passive Jesus to me. In fact, I would say that Jesus has quite a hefty work to get that accomplished before His return.

If Jesus is washing the church with the water of His Word, then we who are called to bring messages to the bride had better double down and really check ourselves if we are truly bringing serious and well-grounded messages in the Scriptures to His bride. He called us to "feed His sheep." Are we doing that, really? Or would the saints instead admit that all they hear from pulpits is a lot of blah blah and more blah?!

We have a *living* and *active* Lord Jesus. So, the question then is, am I listening for His voice? Am I truly searching His Word daily so that out of the fullness of my heart, my mouth will truly speak His messages to His bride?

The saints need more than a correct doctrine about Jesus being resurrected. They need to gather in His name, even if just two or three in number, expectant that He, the living Jesus, will do exactly what He said He would do. **He will show up!** Jesus will manifest His very presence in their midst.

My dad used to say something: "Jesus was accused of many things. But He was never accused of being boring!"

That doesn't mean we need Hollywood-style Christianity. There's already too much entertainment going on in many services. "Lights. Camera. *Action.*" Ugh.

But whenever Jesus showed up anywhere, He knew what to say. He knew what to do. And by both His words and His actions, everyone was utterly amazed!

Jesus hasn't changed. So we need to gather in His name expecting Him to show up and just be Himself. When that happens, say goodbye to dull and dry services!

- - - -

Headless Chickens?

A good friend in Texas read the message I sent out recently called "The Cure for Dry and Stagnant Churches" and then sent back this encouraging reply:

"I finally read 'Cure for Dry and Stagnant Churches.' You hit the nail on the head once again. I feel that what each of us does outside the church doors also shows our 'Dryness Quotient.' My life *is* church and Jesus for those with whom I interact."

So here's what else the Lord gave me along these lines. Hope you too are blessed:

- - - -

Yes, church attendance and involvement should not just be a little add-on, yet for many saints, it seems that's what church is.

As for the church's activities (or proposed activities), we need to dwell upon an image that Scripture gives us, which is as follows:

Jesus is the Head.

And church is the body.

That's found at Ephesians 5:23 and 24.

Did you grow up hearing a frustrated parent say to you at times, "If your head wasn't screwed on real tight, you would forget where you put your hat," or some such comment referring to your head being missing? Sure, we can all become forgetful, whether young or old.

But if in reality one's head for only a moment becomes detached from one's body, you are dead! A news story I read long ago was about a man who was alone in the woods and working with his chainsaw. But in the middle of buzzing away on a log, that tool bucked upward. Those blades cut into the man's neck. Yet he remained conscious.

After tying his shirt around his bleeding neck to try and stop that awful flow, he actually got into his truck, drove himself back to town, and pulled up to the emergency room entrance, where doctors then took over. They successfully reattached that half of his neck to his head. Absolutely incredible! But we all know the story wouldn't have ended that way if the chainsaw accident had actually severed his neck 100%.

Whenever we talk about a certain church, or even a whole denomination, being dead, I think I know how they went from alive to dead. They got decapitated. From that point forward, there is no more lively and functional connection between that church and their headship who is the living Lord Jesus.

Now I will admit to something. Being raised in cities and not much exposed to rural farm life, I had a very unique experience during the five years that I lived in San Antonio, age eight to thirteen.

A friend who lived nearby and I were playing at his house. His name was Harry. And Harry's dad decided that day that it was time to slaughter a couple of guinea hens that had been running around their backyard.

Up to that point, I had never seen any creature deliberately killed other than my dad taking expert aim at pesky flies that would somehow still get passed our screen doors. So once the two hens were caught, Harry's dad put the hen's head upon a chopping block and grabbed a hatchet. With one swift blow, the hen's head was separated from its body.

But the next thing that I saw absolutely amazed me. When the headless hen was released, it spread its wings and flapped madly! It even flew across the backyard and smacked into a large tree trunk and then fell to the ground. All the adults witnessing this just laughed. Two headless hens kept flying around and running into objects like the back of their house or the tool shed.

I asked Harry's dad how this was possible. Shouldn't those chickens just be immediately dead and unmoving right after their heads came off? He said it was just their nerves firing off for a few minutes in spite of being headless.

If a church loses connection to her headship, that being Jesus leading her on what to do and what to say, then what about headless churches? Are the activities that follow going to be just as senseless as those birds I witnessed which flew directionless around that yard?

Are we just doing what we are doing based upon traditions but no longer truly being "led by His Spirit"? Paul said, "All those who are led by the Spirit of God, these are the sons of God" (Rom. 8:14).

In my experience in His fields abroad across thirty-six years now, I would also extend this same kind of questioning toward my fellow foreign fishermen and their agencies. Many activities are proposed and generated by these well-meaning "sent ones." But are we doing what we are doing because we are truly getting our prompting about those things from our living Headship, the Lord Jesus? Or are we just using our creative and fertile imaginations to come up with what we should do next and where and with whom?

One such group had a team based for several years on the island where I live. I had fellowship with several of their workers. Their leader even invited me to teach their members a class for a week, and they seemed quite appreciative of the material I invested into their lives.

Yet I began to notice something about them. Few if any cared about getting involved with any local church. They held their own private chapel services for themselves.

One of their outreach activities was called *street dramas*. By these little public presentations of a simple Bible story or a gospel truth, they considered themselves successful to sow the seed of His Word into those who watched and listened to those little dramas.

So it occurred to me that these workers for the Lord were not prepared for success. If you asked one of them, "So what would you like to see happen after your group puts on one of these dramas?" you would get a blank stare. See happen?

I then had to continue asking them questions, like these: Well, if a man who just watched your drama came up to you and said, "Wow! That really touched my heart. How can I become a follower of Jesus?", what would you do next?

Would you explain the Gospel more clearly to him? Would you help him to pray asking Jesus to become the Lord of His life? And the worker's answers would be, oh sure, I would do that.

Ok, after he prayed with you, what would you do next? Do next? Sure, you have just helped a new soul to become born again, right? So he is now a babe in Christ. Babies are cute but are also quite helpless. They cannot feed themselves nor care for their other needs. They cannot walk nor talk yet. So babies need parenting. Are you going to just walk away from this spiritual newborn and hope he survives?

This is where that worker starts to get nervous. Why? Because where this conversation is heading will lead to a conclusion he has thus far been avoiding, which is, that worker needs to make an ongoing commitment to disciple that newborn.

Then things take on a new level of seriousness when it comes to some practical steps in which new Christians need to be trained. Such as what? How about getting water baptized, finding a local church to commit to in the gathering of the saints for worship, fellowship, and growing in the grace and knowledge of His Word? What about starting the habit of spending time daily in His Book while in His presence?

But if that worker who up to now has been satisfied with a ministry of putting on little street dramas without any concern for successful follow-up on newborn saints, then that worker has come face to face with his own lack of personal discipline in the Lord and his own low opinion about the importance of local church if indeed he is not currently involved with any local flocks. Are they truly youth with a mission? Or more accurately, youth without any maturity?

I wish what I am describing here was rare, but unfortunately it is not. A foreign fisherman whom I will call Roger (not his real name) shifted his family to Penang after nine years of work in a certain Island of Indonesia. I admired that he had experienced more success than me in securing Visas to allow him that long to dwell in that nation because compared to my measly twelve months of life basing in Medan back in 1986–1987, his nine years certainly looked like a great victory.

But as Roger and I became friends, he then told me more and more stories of what he had experienced in Christendom in that Indonesian island east of Java during those nine years. As Roger got to know the local pastors better and better, the more disillusioned he became with them. They lacked maturity. They knew the Scriptures in a minimal way. They were only interested in building their personal kingdoms and reputations. They were more money minded than concerned about the things of God's Spirit.

So Roger had come to a conclusion which I found to be quite shocking. He decided that his work would no longer concern himself with any of the local churches. Instead, he justified hosting private little Bible studies with new converts who would come visit him at his house.

When I invited Roger to accompany me to a service where I was to bring the message in Indo-Malay, he said to me in surprise, "Oh? You mean you are actually working with the local churches here?" I hid my reaction, but inwardly I winced mightily. Yes, he did follow me over to that service and later complimented me on my language skills. But I just found it astounding that the bride of Christ in all of her local forms was so completely rejected and devalued by one of Christ's laborers that He had sent to serve overseas.

Frankly, I will now admit to a litmus test, if you will, concerning any proposed activities for local churches to apply themselves to, or for His workers to do for Him, at home or abroad. It is this: How will this activity contribute to His church to stay connected to the headship of the living Jesus? How will these activities help us grow up and become mature in Him? How will such doings prove that we, His people, are consistently concerned with our obedience to His clear guidance found in His Book?

Paul stated clearly that the goal of his ministry was to bring about "faith unto obedience" (Rom. 1:5 and 16:25–27). How can any church be found in obedience if no longer connected to her headship, the Lord Jesus? How can we say that we love the Lord but justify neglecting or outright rejecting His bride for whom Jesus died?

I will conclude with this story. My father passed away five years ago. During his lifetime, he fulfilled full-time ministry in various churches across thirty-eight years. Not satisfied with that, he went on after retirement to do several more years of interim ministry at two more churches who were between pastors until his health prevented doing any more. For as long as he could, he steadfastly continued to attend and support a local church.

Were all the churches my dad served kind and grateful to him for his diligent work? No, they were not. Two of them had a vocal minority which played politics against my dad, forcing him to leave and find another flock to serve elsewhere.

Were the denominational leaders always diligent to aid my father when he had to deal with church conflicts? Did they eagerly help him to find the next place to relocate to and serve? No. In spite of all of my father's loyalty in all matters to the denomination he grew up in, there were times when dad needed their help badly, but he was just ignored by them.

In short, my dad could have pretty easily justified becoming angry, bitter, and disillusioned to the point of chucking it all out the window. But as I spoke a eulogy at Dad's memorial service, I told them that my dad never gave up on the church. And that kind of steadfastness has left an indelible imprint upon my heart and soul.

The churches of this world are still imperfect. I know that not just in theory, but by experience. I have my share of horror stories I could tell about how I have been treated at times by Christendom, both in my homeland and overseas.

But my dad's example to me was that no matter what, dad would not give up on the local church. So, neither will I.

And especially Jesus will not give up on His promise to keep preparing His bride by the washing of water with His Word. Let every saint and every servant remain committed to stay attached to the headship of the Lord Jesus, not just in doctrinal stance but in real ongoing guidance from Him. Because after all, headless chickens flopping around are really a pitiful sight.

- - - -

More on Martin Luther

After a Texas friend and his wife had read "Headless Chickens" plus watched the 1953 version of the black and white movie of *Martin Luther* on YouTube (which I would encourage any saint to view), we carried on like this today. Hope you too are blessed.

- - - -

Loved that far-reaching epistle!

We watched *Martin Luther* last evening on YouTube. Excellent. That actor reminds me of Richard Burton. I had always thought that Luther was martyred, but apparently he died of a stroke in his hometown.

- - - -

But not 'til he (a former monk) and Katherine von Bora (a former nun) had wed and then been blessed with eight children, six of whom made it to adulthood, but two died in infancy.

There's a couple of other stories associated with Martin and Katherine Luther that I dearly enjoy.

One night, after they had gone to bed, Martin heard a noise, possibly from elsewhere in their home. So Martin got up and tiptoed out of their bedroom to go investigate.

He went down a hallway which led to his office where he wrote and composed many Christian articles, books, and tracts. Then he quietly opened his office door.

As Martin stood in that doorway, who should he see sitting at his desk? It was none other than a manifestation of the devil himself who looked up at him and glared hatefully at Martin's face.

And what did Martin do? He calmly said, "Oh, it's just you." Then he quietly closed the door and went back to bed and slept soundly for the rest of the night!

Martin understood that there was no good reason to get overly excited about his mortal enemy. Why not? Because Martin knew, as should we today, that his enemy is doomed.

But on a different occasion, Martin let his mind get overwhelmed with a number of problems and threats which brought great pressure upon his heart. So he became despondent and depressed for several days.

So one morning, Martin woke up and dragged himself out of bed and shuffled his way to the dining table to await breakfast. Katherine was already up earlier.

But Martin was surprised to see Katherine bring his breakfast to the table while she was all decked out in black, from her shoes to her dress to a scarf on her head and a black veil over her face. She obviously was ready to go out and soon attend a funeral service, but Martin was unaware of any parishioner who had just passed away.

“Woman, why are you dressed like that?” he asked Katherine. She calmly replied, “Oh? Haven’t you heard? God died recently, and I am going to that funeral.”

Exasperated, Martin raised his voice and said, “Woman, you are daft. God did not die!”

And she looked him in the eyes and replied, “Well, the way you have been acting around here lately, you would think that God had died indeed.”

That helped Martin snap out of his depression. For if God is still alive and on the throne, then we still have the God who calls Himself the God of all hope!

\- - - -

Awesome story!

- - - -

Actually, there are two stories. Glad you were blessed!

- - - -

The first one was awesome, and the second one was very human. It's interesting how we can react differently in different situations, sometimes in holiness and sometimes oh so earthly.

- - - -

We have our shining moments when we do and say the right things.

But we are still a work in progress.

You recall an expression that was kinda popular a few years back? It was, "Man, get your act together" or "Now I have got my act together."

But a wiser soul came along and created a bumper sticker whose message has stayed with me. It said

Now that I got my act together,
I forgot where I put it.

After we cross over, we will finally be perfect. But not before then. So says Paul (Phil. 1:6; Rom. 8:29; 1 Thess. 5:23). Yes, amen, Lord.

- - - -

The "Not so Powerful" Genie Joke

A man was on the beach in southern California when he noticed something. The waves were pushing a floating bottle to the shore.

So he walked over and picked it up. There was a cork in the opening. He pulled it out, and to his surprise, a genie comes out of the bottle.

Then the genie bowed to the man and explained, "For releasing me from the bottle, I am allowed to grant you one wish. But you must understand that I am not an all-powerful genie, so your wish must be a reasonable wish."

The man thought for a moment and then had an idea. He said, "You know, I have always wanted to see Hawaii, but I hate to fly. Could you make me a bridge so I could drive myself from California to the Hawaiian Islands?"

The genie looked at the man sadly and said, "Look! I told you already that I am not all powerful. So your wish must be reasonable. Please try again."

So the man became thoughtful. Then an idea came. He said, "You know, I have been married now for a little more than ten years. But sometimes, my wife just frustrates me so much. I cannot figure her out. So could I wish for you to grant me the ability to understand my wife?"

The genie then said, "Did you want that bridge to be two lanes or four?"

- - - -

But Peter did write, "Husbands, live with your wives in an understanding way…" (1 Pet. 3:7).

So I am sure the Lord, not a genie, will make that possible to do.

- - - -

Modern Church Compared to Early Church

In my work of holding seminars with church leaders overseas, across recent years, He has led me to try and bring their attention back to the model of the early church instead of the three models that churches of this era have instead often sought to imitate in their various emphases:

- Governments of the world (which always become more and more complex)
- Businesses of the world (which always focus on money matters)
- Entertainment industry (which always focuses upon giving our natural eyes something else to see)

So churches through their leaders think the ideal to dream and labor toward is producing what we call megachurches who combine all three elements from those three models. Megachurches are indeed very complicated; they focus heavily upon money matters to keep all the wheels spinning and well oiled, and they brainstorm nonstop on how to give the saints something else to see to titillate their natural senses. Sigh.

Can't we do better than this? Can we be more biblical in how we form churches with better forms, functions, and focus? I think the answer is yes, most definitely, and that model is found by going back into the Scriptures and asking our Lord to open our eyes to notice the ways and features of the early church model. To me, she was at least three things:

1. She was simple, not complex.

What did you need at a minimum to have a church in the first and second century? Here's my list. You needed…

Two or three who gathered in His name.

Those few made the same good confession that Peter made about Jesus: "You are the Messiah, the Son of the living God."

A copy of the Scriptures.

The person and leading of the Holy Spirit among them.

And let's add faith, hope, and love.

That's just seven things. And the only tangible items in that list of seven are the Bible and people.

2. The early church was fertile.

Today's churches function very similar to businesses. But the church is not a business. The church is Jesus' bride.

I do not focus upon the various expenses I incur every time my bride needs to go to the dentist or she needs to buy a new dress or a pair of shoes. But any loving hubby will not emphasize about how much she is costing him because he does not look at her like a business that generates profits and losses. He looks at her as his bride.

And when they marry, their mutual hope is that she will be healthy unto fertility so that they can enjoy the fruit of the womb, children. That couple expects to get pregnant, sooner or later.

When I ask pastors today, "Is this church pregnant?", I usually get a puzzled look. "Do we have a pregnant lady in the church?" No, no, that's not my meaning.

The church in Scripture is never called "he" nor "it." The church has a gender and is referred to as "she." Jesus also has gender and is always referred to as "He." Men may appear to be pregnant, but that's just an overly round tummy sticking out. There's no baby inside there.

So since Jesus is male, He will never be pregnant. So whose job is it to become pregnant? That would be the female's task ordained by Heaven.

So when the puzzled pastor begins to follow where I am going, he wonders, "So what would a pregnant church expect to happen?" Well, that's easy. What does a pregnant woman expect to happen after just nine months of pregnancy? A new life within her is developed enough to now come out from inside her and to live separate from her body.

Thus, a pregnant church proves that she is indeed a fertile church. And what is the key thing which will make birthing a daughter church a reality? It is the matter of each pastor having under his wing a "Timothy" whom he is mentoring until the time is right to commission him to go out and to pioneer a new flock, quite possibly with the added blessing of encouraging some of the mother church's members to follow that Timothy to help him succeed.

But when I ask pastors, "Who here is your Timothy?", I get blank stares in reply. If I change one word and instead ask, "Who here is your associate (pastor)?", then I get an immediate answer of either "I don't have one" or "That guy over there."

I can find the word *pastor* in the Scriptures, but I cannot find the term *associate pastor* anywhere in our Bible. So from where does the term *associate* come from? Ahh, that would be the business world, from which we have adopted many of its vocabulary and ways. But the church is not a business—rather a fertile bride.

So this nicely leads into the third feature of the early church.

3. She was reproductive.

One church became two. Later each of them would mature more and then go on to birth two more daughter churches.

So how does a little girl go through that change to become a fertile grown woman, ready to marry and experience the intimacy of the marriage bed and finally to start reproducing? She must be fed, nourished, and cared for by wisdom from above so that she does not remain as a babe or a small child.

So how does this happen to transform from a little girl to a mature woman? It does not happen by what she sees but rather by what she hears. Hollywood entertains us by what they produce for our eyes to enjoy. But our growth in the Lord is not by way of our eyes, as His Word clearly says that "we walk by faith, and not by sight" (2 Cor. 5:7). So how do we come into a growing faith by which we mature? "Faith comes **by hearing** (not by seeing something), and hearing by the Word of God" (Rom. 10:17). Peter also testified that we are to be like babes who long for the pure milk of His Word that by it we may grow and mature (1 Pet. 2:2, 3). Hearing or reading God's Word was a key emphasis in the early church.

I think the churches of this era in modern and prosperous contexts have had enough chances to try and improve on the early church model through all of their complexity, their piles of money, and their showbiz style of worship services. Yet if we are honest, the model of the early church still outshines anything of the modern church.

They were truly taught and enriched regularly by the wealth of truth and wisdom that is found in the Scriptures. They were far more evangelistic and active in sending out servants in missions. They were constantly birthing new churches through their mentored Timothys. And the clincher is, they were ready to face suffering, even death, when persecution arose from time to time while maintaining their faith in the Lord Jesus.

There is much blessing to be found and recovered in the model of the early church. Keep in mind that Jesus isn't just called Shepherd, but rather He is called the Good Shepherd. How do you know if a shepherd is truly a good shepherd?

At the end of the day, a shepherd must gather his flock into a safe enclosure before laying down in the opening to be the *door* to guard them while he sleeps. So they enter one by one, and he counts them, "…97, 98, 99, and…" Huh? That morning, he had 100 sheep. But by 5pm, he only has 99. What does a truly *good* shepherd do at that point? He goes searching for the one missing sheep because that missing one is still valuable to him. Once he finds it, he picks it up and restores it to the flock.

That's what Jesus, the Good Shepherd, is doing, in my opinion, during this age. He is restoring a valuable yet missing element to the ministries of each willing pastor, and that is, each pastor needs to ask Heaven for at least one Timothy. Once granted, then don't send him off to Bible school. No, keep him close by. Be his mentor, just like Jesus mentored His few men who followed Him closely for three years. Pour yourself into that younger saint. Guide and train him about how to care for the flock of God's sheep.

May this become good food for thought for you today.

- - - -

The No. 1 Villain

Paul wrote, "For we have not been given a spirit of fear, but rather a spirit of power, love, and a sound mind" (2 Tim. 1:7).

The *spirit of fear* seems to be Satan's first lieutenant. That spirit is sent to one person at a time but also to incite whole groups, even nations, to move toward their own destruction.

Do you recall the Bali bomb blasts of October 2002? In Bali, Indonesia, a popular tourism spot on the world map, two smaller bombs were set off to cause a herd of humanity to unknowingly head toward a van packed with explosives. Once this third bomb was detonated, it resulted in 202 deaths, and hundreds more badly injured.

What have we just gone through since late 2019 to the present? The spirit of fear was working *overtime* on all the nations of this world. We were made to be afraid of a mysterious virus. We were made to be afraid of getting too close to one another. We were fearful of breathing fresh unfiltered air, so we wore one or more masks the majority of our waking hours. We shouldn't shake hands but just knock one another's elbows or give light fist bumps in greeting. We were told to fear any and all public gatherings, as these were labeled "super-spreader events."

These were the smaller bombs that drove most of humanity toward the bigger bomb.

We were led to conclude that untested and unsafe chemicals that were falsely called vaccines and boosters were the only *safe* way to protect oneself from death, and then those things actually did the opposite and killed many people outright, while others developed debilitating conditions such as unusual blood clotting and myocarditis.

Even Christians often just accepted all of these fears and moved with the masses of humanity in a horrid unity of anxiety. When governments said that the saints were now restricted from gathering for worship services, they mostly just acceded to those demands and thought they were cleverly going to Plan B, called "Zoom meetings," which in reality are *not* meetings at all. At best, they are just another way for His messages to be transmitted to others just like literature or radio or TV or email or websites can do. But they are no substitute for the simple admonition from Jesus that when two or three *gather* in His name, then Jesus Himself will come be in the midst of them (Matt. 18:20). Frankly, the bride of Christ has gotten so far away from the expectation of Jesus being in attendance that if you ask the average church attendee after a service, "What did Jesus do or say today?" you would only get a blank stare as your reply. Huh?

What have we learned through all of these last two to three years? Not only has Satan used fear very effectively to drive humanity toward greater self-destruction, but you can bet the devil has more plans up his sleeve which he will soon unleash upon this world to drive us again fearfully over a cliff.

But what else the saints must recognize is this: If the Lord's perfect love casts out fear (1 John 4:18), then what has our recent track record revealed about our quality of relationship with Jesus on a day-by-day basis? If we spent more time in front of our TVs than in Jesus' presence, then the Communist News Network (CNN) and the British Baloney Corporation (BBC) were not just channels of a bit of anxiety but rather floodgates of fear inundating our souls!

And even if we have gone that way for a long time, what is His remedy? Get back into His presence, and let His fervent love refill our hearts until there is no more room for even the slightest fear.

If we are filled and refilled with His Spirit, which is One of power, love, and a sound mind, then we will recognize what's really going on the next time our enemy launches his next frontal attack with his spirit of fear. We will refuse to join in with the worldly masses who don't know Jesus yet as Lord in their lives. We will resist all the *protocols* that are served up "to keep us safe," knowing that their real intentions for the majority are exactly the opposite. They are not trying to keep us safe. The elites of this world are just maximizing their own insatiable lust for more power over the masses whom they do not esteem as terribly valuable. They think they are smarter than God even though they would not even acknowledge His existence.

So who is it that inspires and influences most of the world's leaders toward those awful goals? Go back and read almost all of three chapters in the Old Testament, called Ezekiel 26, 27, and 28. Together they equal eighty three verses. Only the last seven verses are about God's judgment against a city called Sidon. But the other seventy-six verses are all about the rich city-state called Tyre.

Chapters 26 and 27 describe how rich and powerful Tyre had become. Tyre had gloated over the downfall of Jerusalem, believing that her loss would result in Tyre's gain (Ezek. 26:2). So the Lord predicted quite the opposite would transpire. Tyre would be totally despoiled and destroyed by many nations. The first nation God would support and send against Tyre was Nebuchadnezzar and the Babylonians. Later still, God sent Alexander and the Macedonians to finish up all of Heaven's judgments against her. Tyre would not be able to bribe her way nor fight her way out of the path of destruction for which she was destined by the Almighty.

But as you continue into chapter 28, now the reader notices more about why the Lord is so incensed by Tyre. We first learn of her *leader* in verses 1–10, how he let his heart become so proud that he boasted that he was no longer a man but that he was a god! Oh yes, it was undeniable that this leader gained a reputation as being very wise and clever, and as a result, he had increased his riches greatly. But the Lord foretells that his splendor will be defiled, and he will be executed by his enemies.

But then we arrive at the second figure who occupies a prominent place in the story of Tyre. This is found in the nine verses in 11–19. We find a description of the king of Tyre but soon realize this is no ordinary human king. Twice we find this king also being referred to as a *cherub*, which is a synonymous term for an angel. God refers to this angel as being created, not born as humans are, full of wisdom, beauty, perfection, and innocence until one day, this angel corrupted himself.

He formerly walked in the midst of the stones of fire (most probably meaning he was a holy angel among other holy angels), and he had been both at the holy mountain of God as well as in Eden. But later he ruined his wisdom by reason of his God-given splendor, and thus came under God's judgment. He was cast to the ground and put before the kings of this earth. And God pronounces against this angel that one day, "you will be no more" (Ezek. 28:19).

It does not take a PhD to simply recall who it was that formerly dwelt in the Garden of Eden. Adam was there, and so was his wife Eve. And who else? The serpent, also known as the devil. Jesus testified that He watched the Father cast that defiled angel as a lightning bolt from Heaven to the Earth (Luke 10:18). When the Lord requires Satan to account for his whereabouts, twice Satan replies the same thing: "From roaming around on the earth, and walking around on it" (Job 1:7 and 2:2).

So let's get back to Tyre and her leader who came under God's severe judgment. Why did he allow himself to think and pronounce, "I am no longer a man. I am a god?" Because he was very much under the persuasions of Satan who was the actual king of Tyre.

Has anything changed since the days of Tyre and her complete overthrow? No, Satan still approaches the rich and powerful of this world to use them for his own evil purposes.

And what did Jesus reveal about the heart of humanity's main enemy? He said point blank to those who resisted Jesus and His message that "You are of your father the devil, and you want to do the desires of your father." So what is the devil's number one desire? "He was a murderer from the beginning, and does not stand in the truth, because there is no truth in him. Whenever he speaks a lie, he speaks from his own nature; for he is a liar, and the father of lies" (John 8:44).

Now let's dwell upon that phrase that the devil "was a murderer from the beginning." What was Satan's intention while roaming the earth? Satan was carefully observing this most unique of all of God's creation which was made in God's image and God's likeness, that being the first two humans, Adam and Eve. Was this fallen angel amused by this first man and his wife? Did Lucifer esteem them as the highest of all of God's creation?

No. According to Jesus, Satan was a killer, and he wanted to murder both Adam and Eve. Yet he couldn't touch them as long as they both lived and walked in the original righteousness with which God had made them. So how could Satan contrive an evil plan by which he could kill this man and this woman? His devious mind reasoned, "If I can tempt them to commit sin, then the Lord in His holiness must come and destroy them both."

You may have heard of "suicide by cop." If you want to kill yourself but cannot pull the trigger yourself, then you simply try to provoke the policeman until he shoots you. Well, what Satan had in mind could be called "murder by the hand of the Almighty."

After Eve and then Adam did sin, I don't know if we can fathom the shock that ran through Satan's mind when he heard the following pronouncements from God Almighty. Both Satan himself and the earth came under a curse from the Lord. But the man and woman, though disciplined, were shown mercy. The Lord did not become the deadly weapon which Satan had thought would act against Adam and Eve to execute them. Instead they were promised that a Savior would come forth from the seed of the woman who would one day destroy their mortal enemy (Satan himself), and as a foreshadowing, that Savior would cover their nakedness by His own self-sacrifice. According to Jewish oral tradition, the animals that God chose to slay and give their skins to Adam and Eve to wear were precious little lambs. This would concur with the pronouncement made by John the Baptizer when he saw Jesus and proclaimed, "Behold, the Lamb of God who takes away the sin of the world!" (John 1:29).

My point in all of this is not just to recite sound doctrinal truths. Satan and his murderous desires have not changed across these thousands of years since his fall from Heaven. According to Peter, he is on the prowl like a roaring lion, seeking whom he may devour (1 Pet. 5:8). Peter says that Christians need to be of sober spirit and be on the alert. We are to resist him. The devil is all about death, but our Lord Jesus is all about life!

There are still various kinds of *leaders* today who follow in the footsteps of the leader of Tyre. Those leaders may indeed be very rich, hail from political positions, or even be renowned medical authorities. But if they are not truly disciples of our Lord Jesus who know and follow the Scriptures diligently, then who do you think is the main influencer in their lives?

Years ago, I had a friend who related a sobering story from his own experience. His name was Randy. As a young man, he was trained to become a salesman of a product called waterless cookware.

His company gave him many facts that he could use when giving a sales pitch to any prospective customer as to why they should indeed fork over the money to buy a set of these special pots and pans. Randy was told how different this style of cookware was over the conventional and cheaper stuff out there. If they used less water in food prep, then that meant that all of the diners would receive much more of the natural enzymes, vitamins, and nutrients within the food.

On top of these selling points, Randy was told that these pots had very specially engineered handles. They were guaranteed to never loosen nor fall off of any pan or pot made by this company.

Randy proved himself to be a real go-getter. The number of his sales climbed rapidly. As soon as he had sold a certain number of sets of cookware, Randy was rewarded with a bonus from that company. They gave him a complete set for free!

After a while, Randy and his wife had to relocate. So he left that job and found a different company to work for. But that couple brought with them to their new place all of those special pots and pans and used them daily in their own kitchen.

Then one day, Randy lifted one of those pots off the stove, and to his shock, the handle was very jiggly. Later still, the handle actually came off that pot altogether, and Randy couldn't figure out how to get it reattached.

Then it hit him. How many customers had he persuaded to buy those pots and pans because he told them the *truth* (?) that those handles would never loosen or fall off? Yet now he realized that company had misled him, so he in turn misled all of those who bought those items from him.

That kind of thing can happen over and over today. Authority figures can be under the influence of the "king of Tyre," but they do not realize it yet. And that kind of king has but one desire. He wants to kill as many of us as possible.

I have heard it said that one of the scariest things you can hear today is that after someone knocks on your door, you open it only to hear from the men in front of you, "We are from the government, and we are here to help you." You and I, the saints and the servants of the Lord Jesus, we must exercise discernment when authority figures tell us, "This is for your welfare, for your safety."

The prowling lion is still loose and hungry. The king of Tyre still sits upon thrones today. Point number one inscribed upon the Georgia Guidestones since 1980 says this: "Maintain humanity under 500,000,000 in perpetual balance with nature." Today, there are approximately 7 billion people upon the earth.

Do you understand what the proportions are when those two figures are compared to each other? They are in a ratio of 1 to 14. Put simply, you and thirteen others go into a room, and then eventually one person is allowed to exit said room and carry on with his or her life. But the other thirteen folks? Well, they just need to go away… permanently.

Now who do you suppose inspired that bit of wisdom? The elites of this world do not intend to bring to the masses a future and a hope. Even though someone set off an explosion in July 2022 and tried to destroy those granite slabs and their messages, do you really think that has dissuaded the worldly leaders of today to repent of such death wishes upon humanity? As long as that fallen angel is still loose in this earth, he has but one evil desire. It's called murder. And done on a grand scale, it's called genocide.

If we just "go along to get along," then we may meet the same fate as a large flock of shepherdless sheep in Turkey a few years ago. In 2015, this story made worldwide headlines. As a group of shepherds all went to breakfast together, leaving 1,500 sheep grazing, first one sheep went over a cliff edge, which then was followed by the entire flock.

We need fearless shepherds, not fearful sheep. The spirit that Jesus gives us is not a spirit that leads us to become afraid. His Spirit comes to us with power, love, and a sound mind to discern between a course set on life instead of one set on death.

Satan is our Number 1 villain. The spirit of fear is his first lieutenant. But let us say with David, "Lord, You are our shepherd. So even when we are led through the valley of the shadow of death, we will fear nothing, because You are with us. Your rod and staff will comfort us. You will prepare everything that we need. Your goodness and mercy will follow us always, and we will dwell in Your house forever. Amen." From portions of Psalm 23.

- - - -

Maintaining Humility: How?

After a fellow foreign fisherman saw that photo of me sitting in what seems to be a throne for a Batak King of yesteryear, he cautioned me with the following:

"Stay humble, bro. Stay humble. Yes, all glory goes to Him…! We hold this treasure in earthen vessels, we are only jars of clay."

So the following came up from within, and I hope you too are blessed:

\- - - -

Amen! Not some of the praises, but *all* of them go to our Lord, not to me!

I have been teaching folks at times to compare two verses in Proverbs that start out the same way, but the second half of the second verse then helps to properly interpret what the first verse means.

Both start with, “The crucible is for silver and the furnace for gold…”

Then Prov. 17: 3 says, “but the Lord tests hearts.”

Ok, so how is the purity of silver or gold tested? By using something very very hot to turn it into liquid to then separate the impurities. So the Lord is testing the contents of our hearts using something that is very very hot, but what is it?

Then jump over to Prov. 27:21 to find that answer, which says the following:

“And a man is tested by the praises afforded him.”

So the praises and complements that we, His servants, ever receive are basically normal if the saints or other servants have been blessed by what we have recently said or done or both. “Oh, brother, you blessed my heart today,” or “That really spoke to my current problem. Thank you so much,” and so on. Nothing wrong with that.

What’s wrong is if I ever forget what Paul admitted about himself and is also true for me and every other servant, which is, “In my flesh dwells **no good thing**” (Romans 7:18). But if those folks were truly blessed seemingly by me, what does that mean? It means it wasn’t me doing the blessing. It was

Jesus inside me and through me that was getting something good across to them.

So I exhort His servants that if they want to assure that their hearts remain in steadfast humility before the Lord, then here's what they must do soon after every time they receive praises of men. They must get in the car or retreat somewhere alone and **pass all those compliments onwards to their rightful Owner, that being unto Jesus**.

Say "Lord, did you see all those smiles today? And did you hear all those positive words of encouragement for that message today? But Lord, if it wasn't for You in my life and you teaching me first and then getting those things across clearly to them, what could I do without You? Nothing! So Lord, are you ready? Here they come. I now pass on to You all of those praises because they don't really belong to me. They are Yours. Here Ya go," and then see yourself tossing up to Heaven all of those compliments.

The only One I know who can receive praises **and remain humble** is the Lord Jesus. If any man or woman tries to hold onto the hot praises of men which come our way from time to time, then what happens to your skin if badly burned? You develop scar tissue, which is where your body no longer has any live nerve endings. That means you are now unaware in the future of additional threats to your body's welfare because you cannot feel anything in that part of your body.

So holding on to the praises of men leads us to contract upon our hearts to become covered in more and more scar tissue. In short, your former humility transforms into boastful pride.

I told them here yesterday that pastors sometimes turn into male geese. They looked at me kinda funny when I said that.

But I asked them, “You ever see a goose walking around, especially a gander?” They nodded. “Where is his nose while he walks around? Looking down? Or held high?” They all knew the answer. Ganders strut around with heads held high and their noses to the air, hissing at anyone they don’t like if they come near.

So I imitated how some pastors act whenever they are at a conference with many other servants of the Lord. With my nose pointing up, I started to say, “My flock is bigger than yours, and my worship team has ten musicians, six singers, and eight dancing girls with tambourines and streamers. And I have the latest electronics working in our services,” and so on.

So I told them that when I see such on display, I don’t even need to find out that pastor’s name because I already know it. He is Pendeta Angsa (Pastor Goose).

- - - -

Trying to Teach the Uninterested

A longtime friend in Texas reached me at the start of this trip with a request for help to teach youngsters. Then we had follow-up. Sometimes our fellowship with each other is over frustrations we hold in common. Hope you are blessed to listen in on this chat across a couple of days.

- - - -

"I am teaching the Ten Commandments to four-, five-, and six-year olds tomorrow morning… any hints?"

Sure.

Look up Exod. 25: 21 and 22. Tis about the Mercy Seat on top of God's golden box called the Ark of the Covenant.

What does it say? Moses was told that as he met with the Lord while inside that most holy place where the Ark was, from that place, the place of His mercy, the Lord would give all of His commandments.

So what motivates the Lord to give us various commandments? Because He is mean? No. Because He wants to stop us from having a good time? No.

He gives us commandments because of His kindness and mercy. He wants to keep us safe.

When a mother turns around in the kitchen while cooking and sees her toddler reaching up to touch the hot stove or hot oven door, what does she quickly call out?

Don't touch that!

Why? Doesn't she want her child to grow and explore and learn new things? Yes, she does. But she also wants her child to do all those things *safely*. Her mercy toward her child is great, so that's why she gives commands to her child on what to do and what not do.

I can still recall when those verses caught my eye. A few years back, my bookmark had reached that chapter in Exodus. And I knew it was the start of seven chapters in a row all about the details of the Tabernacle and its required furnishings. My heart just wanted to sigh and skip all that to move on to chapter 32 where more stories awaited.

But inside I heard a gentle, “Ah, ah,” and I realized that He was urging me not to do that, to go ahead and read those detailed chapters.

So I reluctantly started plowing my way through chapter 25, and that’s when He showed me that wonderful emphasis in verses 21 and 22 about how and why the Lord gives us various commandments. He is our God full of *mercy* toward us, His children. Hallelujah!

(The next day)

So ‘tis my Monday morning and your Sunday night now.

How did the lesson go that you taught the youngins?

“As you often probably experience, it was not all I had hoped.”

Oh? Fidgety kiddos?

“No, just my presentation was not all I’d hoped for. The kids were normally squiggly. I tried to do something active to help them remember and have a little fun.”

Yea, I hear ya.

I have had frustrations teaching at Bible schools over here. One time, just outside of Medan, a bunch of young ladies who sat in the back row of over a 100 attendees in that hall kept whispering to each other, giggling occasionally, using their cells to text, showing each other various pix on their screens, and just basically proving to me that they didn't care to listen or learn anything.

So at one point, I decided to lean upon the table where my Bible and notes rested, looked down and stared at my stuff, and went absolutely silent for about thirty seconds. You can imagine that grabbed everyone's attention, including the chatty girls in the back. What happened to the teacher? Did he die mid-lecture?

Then I said clearly and loudly enuf for all to catch it: "The only reason why some of you are in this school is only to find your future spouse."

Then I let that be sink in for a few more seconds of silence that followed.

It had the desired effect, so I could get back to teaching His Word to the eager and hungry ones there without all of that distraction going on.

\- - - -

GO, SEND, OR SIT?

A pastor friend in Malaysia who's been following our updates from our rounds and work in North Sumatra just sent me the following:

- - - -

Long ago, I saw these wordings: go, give, pray. If one cannot go, then give and pray. Even if you can't give, you can still pray (for missions). 😅

You are the goer. I should be backing you at least with my prayer. I suppose the going is the most challenging.

- - - -

So I sent back the following:

Some are called to be the goers, others are the senders, for "how shall they preach if they are not sent?" (Rom. 10:15).

But the third verb of world missions is neither go nor send, but just **sit**. Those are the saints who just passively enjoy that the Gospel somehow reached their area and their people group in their original language but feel no compunction to care about either *going* somewhere for the Lord, nor for helping to *send* someone for the Lord. They just sit.

The only problem with the third verb of world missions is that *sit* cannot be found in His Word. Sitting is not an option for anyone who calls themselves a born-again Christian who supposedly acknowledges Jesus as being their Lord. Our only two verbs which are definitely Biblical are *go* and *send.*

\- - - -

He sent back…

😊 👍 Now we narrow it down to two words.

\- - - -

Amen. Yep, just keeping things simple. 😄

\- - - -

Legalistic Leaders?

A pastor friend in Malaysia responded to the updates I have sent from here in North Sumatra, and he said

“Looks like the people are hungry for His Word.”

So I sent back the following, and I hope you too are blessed… if you don’t choke on it:

\- - - -

Yes, indeed. But frankly, the key person whom I seek to impact is their own shepherd. And hopefully by the end of that message called “Grace Upon Grace,” the closing story will catch in their throats like a chicken bone going down sideways.

When I bring to their attention John 1:17 that says the law came through Moses but grace and truth come through Jesus, I ask them, “Of these two names in this verse, who is more important?” Then they give the correct answer, tis Jesus. Moses didn’t have Holy blood inside him. Moses couldn’t save anyone from their sins.

But when I told them that, I went to the white board and wrote two very large words, those being JANGAN (Don't) on top, and HARUS (you must) below it, and then I turned to the fourteen Bible school students and said, "Next time, it is your turn to prepare a message, for any size gathering, Sunday school, cell group, or even if your pastor turns the pulpit over to you for one Sunday, seek the Lord for a message where **you will not utter either of these terms during that message**.

Why not? Because if you are channeling Jesus more than channeling Moses, then there's no need to exhort the listeners with many Do's and Don'ts because in the New Covenant, we have something better. We have much *grace* and much *truth* to get across.

After all, Heb. 7:19 says something very simple: "the law perfects *nothing*." So what are God's servants accomplishing if we only serve up lots of Do's and Don'ts? Absolutely nothing!

When I told them that the key female leader of the little Bible school heard my suggestion to not use either JANGAN or HARUS in their next message, she became apoplectic! She didn't say it out loud, but if she had, she would have screamed "Mustahil!" (impossible).

That story is a showstopper around these parts of Christendom. But I imagine you knew this already.

- - - -

Back and Forth for Seven Years

"How long did it take you to learn the (Indonesian) language?" asked a West Texas brother.

Well, I have testified about this before, but here is another brief version to answer his question:

- - - -

That's kind of a long story. First, I would say that when you arrive and live in the midst of a people group that is new to you who have their own language, you will have keen incentive *every day* to add to your vocabulary because you want to function, and without local language, you cannot function much at all.

So I had a year living in Medan starting June of 1986, and that gave me a foundation to build upon. But once I had to read the writing on the wall that my efforts to obtain a long-term Visa had failed, I sought the Lord on what to do next.

He showed me that as the door was closing upon me dwelling inside Indonesia, but then there was a door opening to shift the family over to Penang, Malaysia, as our new home base in this region. Since the Brits formerly were in charge of Malaya as it used to be called, then that meant there was widespread knowledge of English, unlike in Indonesia since that nation had been under the Dutch for over 300 years, formerly called the Dutch East Indies.

While getting invitations to serve in various flocks in Malaysia, most of them were using English in their services. So in our first month based in Penang, I picked up my Alkitab (my Indonesian Bible) and put it on a shelf, thinking, "Well, no more need to keep struggling to get my head around this item."

But one month later, I heard the Lord say, "Go get your Alkitab." Oh, ok, Lord.

So for the next seven years, I had my daily quiet time with the Lord using two Bibles at the same time, English on my right and my Indo Bible on my left. Back and forth I would read and study. In this way, the Lord was continuing to build my vocabulary in Indonesian.

By 1994, due to a mix-up on the part of my Medan friend with whom I would travel and who would interpret for me, I showed up to start a two-week tour of duty around this province with him, having first called each of those pastors who were going to set up seminars and revival services for us to lead. But my friend thought the dates were for April, not

March, and he was shocked at my arrival on Friday the 18th of March! He could not go with me!

Now it was my turn to be shocked. You mean, I need to get into the charter taxi tomorrow *alone* without an interpreter to help me for the next two weeks?! Yep, that's what it meant.

So on that Sunday morning, I got into a pulpit with knees knocking a bit and gave it what for—and they understood! Did likewise at a night service, too.

Then on the next three days, for four hours a day, I taught the "Godly Leadership Seminar" to fourteen young adults at a little training center, plus two local pastors also attended, and they too all understood me.

The whole two weeks went like that. When I got home to Penang, I said, "Well, how about that? I guess I have graduated." And ever since, I have not needed to chase down an interpreter partner in this region. All glory to our Lord Jesus!

- - - -

The Texas friend wrote back to say, "That is a common story among those laboring in foreign fields. Their Bibles become their language textbooks, like Holy Rosetta Stones."

- - - -

Grace That Is Greater

A brother in West Texas reached me with the following question:

"Is there a lot of persecution of believers there?"

Here was my reply:

- - - -

Kinda depends on where you mean more specifically and at certain occasions. Certain areas of this nation have a reputation as *hot spots* for M'lim folks. When there is a crisis, economic or otherwise, folks look for some group to blame, to vent their anger and frustrations at something, that is, sanctuaries, or someone, that is, the saints and His servants themselves.

A few years back, a number of sanctuaries got attacked, trashed, ransacked, and so on, in the area of Central Java.

Then an unusual thing happened a few months later. A number of men fell sick or very weak. When they sought treatment from a Christian doctor, his examination of each man did confirm that something was indeed wrong with them. But the doctor could not put his finger on the cause from a medical point of view.

I guess that doctor got inspired from above to then start asking each of them a rather unusual question for a doctor to ask. He queried, “Were you part of those gangs a few months ago who attacked several churches?” Most of those men were willing to admit, yes, they had participated in all of that destruction.

Then the doctor counseled them like this: “If you want to get well, I think you need to go find those pastors and tell them you are sorry for what you did and then ask them to forgive you.”

As this story goes, quite a few were suffering enough that they really wanted relief. So they humbled themselves, sought out those pastors, and asked to be forgiven.

The pastors did more than forgive them. They laid hands upon them (with their permission) and prayed for them in the clear name of Jesus that Jesus would heal them.

Then that’s what happened. They got healed, and this made them very curious to learn more about this man called Jesus. As I heard, many then repented and accepted Jesus as their Lord. And they no longer ravage church property.

That story reminds me of Paul's statement which says, "For where sin increases, grace can more greatly abound" (Rom. 5:20).

\- - - -

To All Salt Lovers

A good friend in the Dallas area reached me with some thoughts and questions from his study about salt in The Book. So to all of my fellow lovers of salt, I present the following, which he later told me was helpful. Hope you too are blessed:

- - - -

Brother, I was studying yesterday and came across a passage in Lev. 2:13, "You shall season all your grain offerings with salt. You shall not let the salt of the covenant with your God be missing from your grain offering; with all your offerings you shall offer salt."

It made my thoughts go in another direction just wondering about something. These offerings that are spoken of here are the offerings that the book of Hebrews speaks of that the priests would make over and over yet they could never pay for our sin. Also, the word says that these things are a shadow of what was to come.

We know Jesus came to save the world. And He is the perfect sacrifice, the lamb of God who takes away our sin.

Then I read of Jesus telling his disciples that we are the "salt of the earth." I also noticed that the Word mentions "salt covenants."

Is there any connection between God requiring salt with every sacrifice/offering and Jesus calling us the salt as He makes the perfect sacrifice? I don't want to make wrong assumptions brother. Thanks.

- - - -

I usually take the simplest and most direct route when certain passages seem to require that we seek to properly interpret them.

So…

Has anyone ever served you green beans that they cooked but forgot to salt them first? Bleah!

And then don't you quickly ask someone to pass you the salt so you can anoint said blah beans with a generous dose of salt? Big difference in flavor, right?

Salt makes food much more interesting and enjoyable. Salt also has a necessary nutrient within itself so that if salt intake becomes minimal, then it causes a thyroid condition called a goiter.

So it doesn't seem like a big leap to me to ask any saint after they walk out of a service, "How was the message today?" And if they cannot hardly recall what was said from the pulpit, then it seems to me that you were served a "spiritual meal" which had little or no seasoning, especially salt.

In short, *where were the stories* that should have been sprinkled into that meal? If there are no illustrations to clarify and to apply those truths, truisms, and wise sayings to our lives from a servant (a cook, if you will) who himself has already experienced those things, then yes, that meal can give you some sustenance, but food that is blah just doesn't endear itself to our palate.

Jesus told stories. So did others who we esteem highly in The Book.

I personally feel like that as the Lord is starting to show me something, that before I launch out to try and serve that food to others, that I first need the appropriate stories to go alongside *each point in that message*. You cannot just season once while cooking.

- - - -

Coping and Overcoming in Him

A sister in Malaysia who kept up with all of our updates and news from our twenty-six days of service in Indonesia just sent the following:

"Happy to hear that you both are back to Penang safely. It was a fruitful trip. Praise the Lord."

So as a bonus, I just related how things went on our last day and transition back to Penang. Hope you enjoy this item also:

- - - -

Amen.

Yesterday morning included the task to try and pull money from a Medan ATM and, if successful, step inside that bank and make a deposit into a pastor's acct to complete the total needed for the project to put in a ceiling in the village church at Banuaji.

God gave success on both counts though it meant wrestling with the idiosyncrasies of several ATM machines in that room. Three of eight machines were out of order. Two wouldn't give me as much per pull as I wanted. Then they said they were out of cash.

Then that Malaysian card wouldn't work for any more withdrawals. So I said, "What now, Lord?" He reminded me that I hold another card that is part of my American bank account. Oh yea! I then shifted to another machine and finally got the full amount needed.

Once deposit was made, I took a pic of the receipt and then texted that pic to that pastor as proof he now has the money. He texted back his great gratitude for that help.

It was a full morning before I ran back to our hotel room, showered off the sweat, changed outfits, finished closing bags, and then had late checkout at 1 pm. Then we were taken to the airport an hour away to get checked in.

While awaiting our turn, it sounded like WW3 was about to erupt from a nearby check in kiosk. First, one lady was seen and heard raising her voice and obviously very angry. Uniformed security started showing up and standing nearby in case it was time to stop or break up a fistfight. Then another lady got into the same act. More security showed up.

Thankfully all our stuff was in order, and we got checked in without incident.

Then had a late lunch of goat curry over rice before we went thru security and immigration. No problems processing back into Penang. Whew! Thank you, Lord!

- - - -

His Thoughts Help Me Cope

The following came to me six days after learning of my daughter's recent suicide:

I will confess that I need help with my thought life when it comes to all of this mess in relation to the disposition of Jennifer's body. I will hold on to hope that my request of Heaven to send back her spirit can still happen right up to the graveside service after the funeral so that we could all witness the sound of knocking from inside the closed casket and a voice calling out to open this box.

But if Heaven has a different answer, and that doesn't happen, at times, I find myself having an argument with her corpse about how inconsiderate it was of her to choose to end her life at that particular time period. Forensics may very well determine that her death happened on the 4th, the last date that Michael (her husband) and I both got our last texts from her, which happens to be her favorite sibling's birthday, that being when Stephen in Japan turned forty. So did she want to inflict Stephen whom she loved so much with an annual reminder on his future birthdays that that was when she ended herself? What a gift!

Then there's the matter of her body being carried off by government authorities to perform autopsy and do toxicology reports… oh but wait. The federal holiday of Veteran's Day would add more delays to getting this stuff done. So now we the living all wait and wait in limbo as to when her body will be released and then finally all of us can get a firm date set up for her funeral in Colorado, which is a spot on the map where *none* of her family dwell; so that fact gives rise to how all of her family must figure out how to do backflips in order to make plans to drive that far on short notice to attend said funeral and graveside.

Oh, by the way, we are coming up on the annual season of the Thanksgiving holiday, so what shall we all do? Put a turkey bird on a table somewhere or just forsake such because we all must use our time to travel to and from Colorado by car?

Like I said, these awful thoughts climb up in my head from time to time, demanding answers and no answers are yet forthcoming.

But in my saner moments, His Word tells me that "no man hates his own flesh but nourishes and cherishes it." So whenever we get the terrible news of someone who has deliberately ended (or attempted to end) his or her life, it tells me one thing. That is *not* how our Maker made each one of us. He made us to desire to give proper care each day to the welfare of this house we each one live inside which are called our bodies.

So then this leads me to conclude that every act of suicide indicates that there is something *demonic* in the mix, for as Jesus said, "the thief comes only to steal *and kill* and destroy…." Killers have no concern whatsoever for how inconsiderate is the timing of their dastardly acts.

I told both churches that I served yesterday an insight that the Lord had just brought to me while having breakfast before we headed to the first service an hour away. The Lord reminded me of the famous story that we call The Valley of Dry Bones.

Since three years ago, He opened my eyes so that I now teach from time to time about what is needed for real revival in any church or denomination from the three steps to which Ezekiel was witness to make that tremendous transformation take place from a huge collection of dried out human bones to then become a living and revived strong army for the Lord.

The Lord got me to consider what does it mean when Ezekiel first arrives at that valley and sees human bones jumbled and scattered as far as the eye can see. What that prophet is looking at are the pitiful remains of a large army *who has suffered a catastrophic defeat*. Their hateful enemy had not only killed all of those who opposed them, but in their vindictive state of mind, they cared not one whit for the proper disposal of all those dead soldiers. No burials took place. "Just leave them to the wolves and hyenas and vultures and finally the blow flies."

Now what happens when those predatory critters converge upon this huge feast of corpses? Do they dine elegantly and with proper manners? Of course not. They are at times snarling at each other as they fight over favorite portions that they want to sink their fangs or claws into. Bodies are being literally torn apart. Once the last bit of marrow has been consumed by the insect world and there is absolutely nothing left to eat, now these many scattered bones just get bleached under the hot sunshine day by day.

That is the starting point for the vision given to Ezekiel. He shows up to witness not a large collection of properly laid out individual human skeletons but rather a scene of such carnage and chaos that I am impressed all over again with that prophet's response to the Lord's question, "Son of man, can these bones live?" And he properly answers, "Oh Lord God, You know if that is possible."

So here's the bottom line. Sometimes our enemy finds a way to wreak total death and destruction *upon God's army*. But because all things are possible with our Lord, guess what shocker awaits our enemy and his forces who have long left that field of battle and who have smugly scorned God's people as being of no threat and no account?

The noise and the battle cries are once again arising from His people who are marching fearlessly toward Satan and his minions. "Yes, Satan, you did win a battle, but you did *not* win the war. And we the revived ones are now coming for you again. Only this time, let's see who leaves the battlefield victorious!"

- - - -

Pigs or Guinea Pigs?

This topic of dealing with one's grown children, especially when Christian dads and moms witness that their sons or daughters are not now walking with the Lord in spite of how they were trained in a godly household, has generated some significant exchanges of messages. So I hope what follows blesses and edifies every reader as we truly seek to fulfill our God-given stewardship to be godly parents who still want to help and bless our sometimes wayward adult children:

- - - -

After a brother in Oklahoma read "His thoughts help me cope," he sent back the following:

"Truly God inspired my brother. Even through this difficult time, you are a godly example and inspiration. My wife and I continue to pray for you and your family. GBU."

At this moment, what comes to mind is what Peter reminisced about concerning Jesus during His time of suffering and great humiliation in His last hours, found at 1 Pet. 2:20–23. Jesus set the example for us in His worst and most difficult and painful time of His entire life upon this earth. When reviled, He did not revile in return but just kept entrusting Himself into the Father hands.

But I don't mind admitting that I am indeed allowing room in my thoughts for directing threats against the real enemy in all of this mess. "Satan, you won this round, but before the last round is done, *you will be done forever, along with your lieutenant, death, who will go into the lake of fire with you! So, happy trails, my enemy!*"

- - - -

For years, my wife and I have lived with the knowledge that we could lose our son the same way at any time.

The enemy has tried using this fear on me many times, and many times he was successful. When I shared the sad news about Jennifer, the first thing my wife said was, "I wonder who will be next." I tried to encourage and remind her what the Lord reminds me when I struggled with such thoughts. We have no choice but to trust Him. He has a plan, and it's a good one.

Fear is a primary tactic of the enemy but he will not win. He is already defeated!

- - - -

My good friend, a former roommate both in college years and one year of seminary together, and I talked at some length the day after I got this terrible news. He too and his wife have great concern for their two grown sons, knowing that they did indeed "train them in the way they should go" in accordance with Prov. 22:6 and other passages about godly parenting.

Yet where those two sons are in life now is a great temptation to worry about their fate. They are not presently walking with the Lord, and their track record during their young adult years is nothing for any Christian to admire.

But through my tearful voice, I told him the following which sounds like it could also apply to you and your spouse:

When and where possible, you must get in their faces and tell them point-blank what happened to my Jennifer and then add, "Son, there is no substitute for calling out to Jesus! No drugs, no group of friends, no successful career, nothing and no one can take the place of knowing and walking with Jesus as your Lord. Without this, *you are headed to destruction*, not just during this life upon earth, *but forever*."

- - - -

Good wisdom. But if they accepted Jesus at some point in their life, is their Salvation not guaranteed?

- - - -

You are my good friend and brother in our Lord. So I have no interest in trying to be hard on you when it comes to this delicate subject.

So look at a few verses, and more could be found and added later, which speak to this important topic:

…Jesus was faithful as a Son over God's house, whose house we are, *if we hold fast our confidence and the boast of our hope firm until the end.* (Heb. 3:6)

…Jesus became to all those *who obey Him the source of eternal salvation…* (Heb. 5:9)

…that if you confess with your mouth *Jesus as Lord* (not declare just that He is the Savior or even your Savior), and believe in your heart that God raised Him from the dead, *you shall be saved.* (Rom. 10:9)

I believe that Christendom in general, in our eagerness to evangelize and thus to increase our ranks, we have short-circuited the true and clear message of the Gospel to the not-yet-saved world, that is, we have sold folks on the idea that all you need is Jesus as Savior. So just making a confession of faith in Him and/or praying a sinner's prayer are enough to accomplish that goal.

But the key word out of John the baptizer's mouth at the start of his public ministry, plus same for Jesus after His temptation, plus that of Peter on Pentecost when the hearers called out to him, "So what must we do to be saved?—all three used the same single word: **repent**!

Repent of what? Repent of carrying on with your lives with *you in charge of your life* because you have proven that with you as lord and calling the shots, that you are a *lousy* lord. You keep choosing sin and the ways of sin, whether it be the truly wicked kinds of sinning, or else the more deceptive kind which is the delusion of self-righteousness, *which does not exist*."

To become a real Christian involves this necessary recognition that I am not a good lord, but the good news is, there is One, and only One, who truly is a good, righteous, holy, and wise Lord, and that is the person of the resurrected (and therefore living) Jesus. So genuine repentance involves at its core that I must reliquish the lordship over my life to the Lord Jesus and that *this new kind of relationship must continue throughout the remainder of the time period appointed by Heaven for me to be upon this earth* before He calls me to my eternal heavenly home.

If you find a pig almost drowning in deep mud in his favorite pigstye, yes, you can go out out there like any concerned farmer would be for his prized pig, bring a rope, and get all filthy in the process of rescuing said pig from his deadly dilemma. Then once clear of the mud, the farmer says to himself, "My my, what a mess you have made of yourself."

So he gets inspired. He grabs the hose and a scrub brush and gets busy to release the pig from all of that caked on mud. Then he gets another idea. He goes inside and comes back with two items, a red hair ribbon from his wife's dresser, which he ties in a bow around the pig's neck, and his own bottle of Old Spice, which he applies liberally upon the body of said pig.

Wow! What a transformation! This clean and good smelling critter is now ready to enter the competition at the next county fat stock show.

And to the farmer's consternation, once the tied-up pig is released from the rope that held him in one place while the pig's *savior* got the pig all squeaky clean, to where did the pig make a beeline? Yep, right back into all of that muddy pit which had endangered his very life just a short time before!

Why? Why does the pig do so? Because the nature of the pig's heart is to enjoy mud, even if that same mud might drown said pig.

If that farmer had power to not just pull the pig out of the muddy pit but then to change that creature from being a pig to instead become a guinea pig, would a guinea pig enjoy diving into a pile of mud? Absolutely not! And I know this for certain, having enjoyed a pet guinea pig for six years in my childhood.

Guinea pigs like to keep themselves clean. They preen. They give themselves frequent tongue baths.

So yes, you might get a sinner to temporarily become ashamed enough of his sins for him to then call out for the Lord to forgive him. And what will the Lord do? He will forgive that sinner. In fact, the Lord likes to forgive!

But then what will that freshly forgiven sinner go and do next? Since his heart hasn't yet been changed, then like that farmer's prized pig, the sinner just goes and plunges into all of the same sins for which he had just gotten forgiveness.

Lord is not meant to be a hollow title nor just an honorary title to be placed in front of Jesus' name. Jesus said once, "Why do you call Me 'Lord, Lord,' **but you do not do what I say**?" (Luke 6:46). So Jesus does not think that we are giving honor to Him just because we say He is the Lord Jesus *if we do not truly listen to Him and then seek to follow His leading in this life*.

All of this does not mean that I personally know how to adjudicate the eternal status of any so-called Christian who seems to have a track record that doesn't look or sound very Christian to me. That is above my pay grade, and I am no one's judge about their current eternal destination.

But I would be remiss in my heavenly assigned duties to just tell worldly folks that all they need to do is just "receive Jesus as their Savior." They need more than forgiveness. They need to get under new management. That's the simple message that needs to get across.

- - - -

Much to meditate on there, and I appreciate your godly wisdom. He knows our hearts. And I'm thankful and grateful for that. Before the Lord saved me, I begged and pleaded for His forgiveness *many* times. Numerous actually. It wasn't until I truly accepted Him as my Lord and Savior that I received my new heart. Prior to that I'm sure I believed I was *saved.* I look back and understand now that that was not accurate. My prayers are that our grown son really accepted Jesus as his Lord and Savior as well.

- - - -

I also love the verse found at John 1:12, which declares,

"…but to as many that received Him (the Lord Jesus), to them God gave them (the repentant ones) the power to becomes sons of God, even unto them that believe upon His name (the name of the Lord Jesus Christ)."

Yet how are we to explain that there are quite a few who supposedly did this, that is, they said that they had "received Jesus," yet the way of their lives, their bad choices, and their addictions or bad habits are not changed for the better? Why not?

And as best I understand now from His Word, their understanding of "receiving Jesus" had little or nothing to do with the message of repentance.

"Repent? Of what? I am no great sinner who murders or rapes or robs banks. Now those kind of folks, yes, they indeed need to repent."

This is why I often lift up an often overlooked verse found in Paul's letter to Timothy, which goes like this:

"The sins of some men are quite evident, going before them to judgment; but for others, their sins follow after." (1 Tim. 5:24)

In other words, there are two kinds of sinning, which are those overtly wicked acts which both Christian and non-Christian tend to agree with each other in assessing those things as "terrible wickedness." But there are other kinds of sinning that seem to be much less hideous to our way of thinking, like telling white lies or taking home a few office supplies from where we work. I mean, c'mon, it's no big deal, we often say.

But the Scriptures do not say "The wages of *big* sinning is death, but the wages of little sinning is, well, don't worry about it, you can still get into Heaven's backdoor later." No. It says, "The wages of sin is death" (Rom. 6:23), that is, eternal separation from your Maker and all of the blessings that are in His presence. So if we get what we deserve, guess what we all deserve? Death, because "all have sinned" (Rom. 3:23).

Go into church history. Look at any form or manifestation of Christendom. When Jonathan Edwards, a Congregationalist in the 1700s, preached his famous message called "Sinners in the hands of an angry God" and he called upon churchy members to repent, what happened? God blessed with a tremendous revival and many got saved.

When circuit riding Methodist preachers in the 1800s boldly told their listeners to repent, what happened? God blessed those messages, and many came to the Lord in humble repentance. Same can be said for the preachers in the Restoration Movement and for the Southern Baptists and any other group too. The Pentecostals at the turn of the twentieth century did likewise, and again God blessed those calls to repentance, and many indeed repented and got saved.

But what happens every time soon after these moves of God Almighty break forth? There's the devil, waiting in the wings, observing, seeking his opportune time to slip into those churches and their Bible schools and seminaries to begin to water down that clear message to repent. Those denominations became over time more and more liberal minded to the point that it became extremely rare for any of their leaders, preachers, and bishops to even utter the word *repent*.

And so what happens to such churches who no longer call on people to repent? Heaven quits blessing them. Fewer and fewer ever get saved. The messages are so watered down that folks don't really know what is the genuine gospel message.

Gospel? Means good news? As compared to bad news? What bad news? Why, aren't we all God's children on our way to Heaven one day? Surely a loving God would never send any soul to a Christless Hell, now would He?

So now we have whole denominations who never mention repentance because there is no need for that topic. Live any way you want, and call yourself a Christian if you care to. But even if you don't, it doesn't really matter because all of humanity is on its way into the arms of a loving God.

The early church understood the importance of the message of repentance. If we today in Christendom, no matter what branch or tradition of it that we were raised in, truly want to see a great influx of new souls becoming truly saved and walking obediently with Jesus as their living Lord, then this basic message must be recovered. There is no substitute for calling folks, en masse, or one by one, to repent, both of their sins, but also of their own lordship over their lives.

As Jesus said, "No man can serve two masters." You cannot truly have Jesus as Lord in your life while also trying to retain your own Lordship over your life. That would be like unto having two masters, two lords.

Jesus is not sitting upon a couch. Couches are made for two or more people to share at the same time. No. Jesus sits upon a throne, and a throne is made for only one derriere at a time.

So whose backside is upon your throne? Yours? Or Jesus'? You cannot have both sharing that throne. If you are still running the show in your own life, then it's time to hear the message to repent, to get off that throne, and to invite Jesus to take your place as being in charge of all of your big decisions in life and many of the lesser ones as well. It is time to repent.

- - - -

Yes, I agree 100% that repentance is critical. It's so critical to me that I do it often.

But for someone that accepted Jesus in the past and asked for forgiveness and repented but, down the road, walked away or turned their back on the Lord, are they destined for separation from God in Heaven?

- - - -

Judas Iscariot agreed to become a follower of Jesus. He was one of the inner group of twelve disciples. He was chosen to be entrusted with the funds that were generated from Jesus' ministry.

But Scripture calls him "the son of perdition." And I just looked up the definition of perdition. Here it is:

(In Christian theology) a state of eternal punishment and damnation into which a sinful and impenitent person passes after death.

If we find that statement to satisfy us, then what is the conclusion to draw about Judas? Does Christendom at large expect to see Judas in Heaven? Methinks not.

Jesus had His Judas, and Paul had his Demas. Paul's latest statement on that man who formerly worked alongside Paul in ministry, but later he fell away completely. Paul said of him, "Demas has forsaken me having loved this present world" (2 Tim. 4:10). Sounds to me like Paul didn't expect to find Demas in a Heaven.

What about those shocked "servants of the Lord" who get locked out of Heaven? Jesus talked about them in Matt. 7:21–23.

What about the parable of the ten virgins, five of whom were wise and five were foolish? Did they all get into the wedding feast when the bridegroom finally showed up? No, the foolish got locked outside (Matt. 25:1–13).

We are told to "work out your salvation with fear and trembling" (Phil. 2:12). It is the most serious subject one can apply oneself to fulfill in this life. So let us not become flippant about what does it truly mean "to be saved."

- - - -

Hmm… Much more to chew on. The topic of Judas is one I've pondered in the past as well. But based on Scripture, I too will be surprised to see him in Heaven. I have tended to view the topic of Salvation more "black and white." Your insights introduce a lot more gray in my mind. For our son, I will pray that the Lord continues to pursue him until his last breath. Covering all the bases so to speak.

- - - -

Yea, I hear you, my brother.

- - - -

Whose Priority: His or Ours?

It just so happens that both in the United States and in our overseas home of Malaysia, national elections were held this month. And for so many saints in both nations, the election outcomes were a great disappointment. Much had been hyped, not just by secular commentators but also by very inspired brethren who had prognosticated big wins that would indeed benefit His flocks.

So when a brother in Penang sent word of how disillusioned he and many others had become, the following is the reminder which I felt came to me from Above to relate to him (and indeed, he wrote back with a hearty *amen*). Hope your hearts are also revived according to His Word and His way:

- - - -

What did Jesus talk to His men about across those forty days after His resurrection? Kingdom of God (Acts 1:3).

On the 40th day, just before He ascended to Heaven, what did His men ask Him about? Restoring the Kingdom of Israel (Acts 1:6).

Has anything changed much in 2,000 years since that day? His people keep trying to shift the focus from Kingdom of God stuff to kingdoms of men and earthly politics stuff.

Since Jesus does not change, where are we supposed to maintain our focus? I rest my case.

- - - -

POLITICS: THE SOURCE OF PEACE?

That last brief note has prompted several positive replies. Then the Lord reminded me of the following truths. Hope the former appetizer has whet your palate for some meat and potatoes now:

- - - -

I recall a certain story that came up after Pat Robertson tried but failed (in 1988) to gain the nomination as the Republican Party's nominee to become the next president after Ronald Reagan's second term came to a close. Instead, George H.W. Bush went on to become the next president.

But when Pat was being interviewed after that campaign failed to secure the nomination, he said something that has stuck in my mind ever since. Pat reflected that he had heard time and again from devout Christians all across the United States that if the saints could just help push Pat successfully to cross the finish line, not just to become the nominee but, further, to become the next president of the United States, then *all* of America's problems would get solved from the top down by his beneficent edicts. In short, Pat said that Christians thought Pat would be elected to become **an all-powerful king** instead of becoming a president who would still have to navigate his way between the three branches of American government. Pat realized that most voting Americans **are monarchists at heart**.

Yet from the inception of the new nation of America, the first potential ruler, General George Washington, thoroughly rejected the proposal that he himself should ascend a throne and become America's first king. Basically the two George's were of opposite mentality.

The George back in England thought he had the right as a ruling king to act like an absolute dictator over the unruly American colonists. But the George over in America didn't even trust in himself to not become like that other George if he too should agree to become America's first king.

There will come a day, it is already marked into the Divine Day Planner, when King Jesus will come back to earth, and He will begin a full thousand years of His wise and beneficent rule over this entire earth. There will not be a single remote outpost of humanity anywhere who will be unaware or unaffected by His millennial rule.

And all of humanity, every tribe and tongue and culture, will be very blessed indeed, for He is righteous, and it will be a rule fulfilled in complete righteousness. No more favoritism for one group over another. No more schemes of the powerful to bribe their way to fulfill their own selfish ways. No more unfairness of any kind. Jesus will rule with a rod of iron. That means, from then on, it will be the Jesus way or the highway. No ifs, ands, or buts about it.

It's fine for the saints of today to dwell upon those prophecies of wonderful things to come. They might even begin in our lifetimes. Wouldn't that be exciting? It kinda makes me giggle with joyful anticipation.

But until that specific day is reached which has been determined by our Heavenly Father (Acts 1:7), the focus of the saints is to be upon the Kingdom of God. Before Jesus comes in the future to rule this world with a rod of iron, He wants to come *now* as the ruling Lord and Shepherd within the hearts of as many souls who will yield to His Lordship in quiet submission. That is to be our main message to the not-yet-saved—that is the mission set before us by our Lord Jesus.

Yes, we can be involved to some degree in the politics of our day and of our location on the world map. Jeremiah sent word to his fellow Jews who had already been forced into exile in faraway Babylon to do so: "Seek the welfare of the city where I have sent you into exile, and pray to the Lord on its behalf; **for in its welfare, you will have welfare**" (Jer. 29:7).

But please, let us, His people, come back to clear thinking about what is our priority. Let us leave behind a concept of blending the Kingdom of God with the machinations of the kingdoms of this world. Those are two separate things. They are *not* joined at the hip.

And while we let ourselves hope and believe that those two things can be united together before the second coming of Jesus, then we are just setting up our souls for more disillusionment, despair, discouragement, and disgust when we don't see the political results turn out the way that we want. It is little wonder that so many saints find themselves lacking His peace and His joy in these recent days and weeks.

What's the solution? Turn off the TV, the radio, and the Internet. Then grab your Bible (if you can find it), blow off the dust, and then pray, "Lord Jesus, please open my eyes that I might behold wonderful things in Your Word," which kinda sounds like the prayer in Psalm 119:18. While you spend time in The Book, keep in mind that you are also spending time in His actual presence with you. Open the eyes of your heart, and "see" what cannot be seen with natural eyes just yet (2 Cor. 4:17, 18). See Jesus. Look into His face. Does He look worried like many shocked and saddened news commentators as they deliver very sobering election results?

That's not what I see. I see Jesus calm, confident, and smiling. When He said on His last night with the eleven (Judas had already left the room), "My peace I give to you," He wasn't kidding (John 14:27).

But He didn't stop there. He compared His gift of peace with the way this world doles out peace: "...not as the world gives, do I give to you." Meaning? His men did not need to wait until those pesky idolatrous Romans were defeated either politically, militarily, or both, nor for those legalistic Pharisees and the licentious Sadducees to be banished from the Temple and the synagogues to finally enjoy some measure of worldly peace. So, let's finish that verse: "Let not your heart be troubled, nor let it be fearful." Why do we let ourselves get so caught up in politics, whether it be in national affairs or in church hierarchy?

I watched my father, a pastor of more than thirty-eight years of full-time ministry, get slammed down more than once by the doings of church politics. It was not a pretty sight. Looking back, I become more amazed that somehow my Dad kept going in church ministry all of his life. It must have been the Lord who helped him each time that happened to get his focus turned back again to Jesus Himself.

Yes, it will be quite wonderful and very glorious when Jesus comes back to rule this world for a thousand years. But until that Heavenly ordained time period is set to begin, let's just double-check that Jesus is now on the throne of our hearts and ruling in all the affairs that concern our daily lives. When that kind of intimacy and obedience are maintained, then somehow the peace and joy that He wants to give us are indeed steadily flowing into our souls.

- - - -

Miracles or the Lack Thereof

In the days following the sad news of my daughter's death, there were several thoughtful exchanges when my brethren learned of my request that her spirit be sent back to her, which did not happen. This is not an easy subject to deal with, that being about miracles or the lack thereof.

- - - -

A pastor in Texas texted me:

"May the Lord comfort you with His grace at a difficult time!"

- - - -

Thanks much. Comfort is a great thing, and so is His grace, which He calls us to be strong in. I have recently been teaching from 2 Tim 2:1 by which Paul exhorted that younger servant of the Lord to do so.

But I don't want to just move on from here without more answers from above about this matter, and my encouragement from His Word tells me that in Jesus is grace **and truth** (John 1:17). So I want to know the truth about the presence or the absence of His power.

But not because I am seeking to obtain some kind of high status within Christendom. I don't need a reputation as a powerful miracle worker.

I am content with my calling to simply be a teacher of His Word in the body of Christ anywhere He sends me. Methinks all of His servants today should ask ourselves from time to time if we can honestly make the same confession that John the baptizer made when he told his own disciples, "He (Jesus) must increase, but I must decrease." All of the miraculous acts of Jesus did exactly that. His name got magnified more and more.

In the days of Amos, he predicted a very terrible famine that would come one day. But that famine would not be a lack of food or water. It would be a famine of not hearing a word from the Lord for a long, long time, and people would travel far and wide, seeking to find someone, anyone, who had heard anything of late from Heaven, but they would encounter no one with a fresh Word from above (Amos 8:11–13). And thus they would languish during that famine since man does not live by bread alone **but by every Word which proceeds**

from the mouth of our God. This is what Jesus quoted from Deuteronomy to Satan while being tempted (Matt. 4:4).

But where oh where is the prophecy that predicts **a famine of His great power**? I read, study, meditate, and at times even memorize portions of His Word. By this point in my life, tis safe to declare that I have a pretty good working knowledge of the Scriptures from Genesis to the maps (which you know are printed after you finish Revelations).

But maybe, in spite of all of the time that I put into daily going through The Book, just maybe, I have missed something on this topic about our God's limitless power. So please, I urgently request your aid or any other of my brethren in Christ Jesus to help me out here. I sincerely desire more answers, more truth.

Even if what I long for does not arrive under my eyes before I leave this world for my Heavenly home, I am persuaded that *all* answers await me on the other side. Because in the Love Chapter, brother Paul wrote this: "Now we know in part, but then (i.e., on the other side in His presence) we shall know **fully** even as we have been fully known (1 Cor. 13:12).

- - - -

Another friend in Texas sent me a thoughtful response about this matter of evident miracles:

I don't know if you can watch the 700 club or have the CBN News app. They have reports almost everyday on miracles that happen to people. On the 700 club broadcast they pray for healing miracles daily and read messages from listeners who have had or seen miracles.

- - - -

My reply:

Yes, in times past, I have followed some of the programs on 700 Club.

I can tell you that across the years, I have witnessed odd things going on within sectors of Christendom who say that they believe in the power of God to perform "signs and wonder." Yet in their eagerness to be involved personally with His power in an evident way, what have some leaders resorted to?

They call folks forward to be prayed for (ok, that's fine so far), but then hands are laid upon him or her, and loud praying commences, along with some dramatic pushing upon the forehead, which results in someone being "slain in the Spirit." The person usually cooperates by falling backward, and normally there are assigned "catchers" behind the one being pushed over. And if this phenomena gets repeated over and over, person by person, with the floor space getting filled up with these "holy corpses," then those leaders boast that during that service, there was truly evident "the power of the Lord."

Hmm...

Don't get me wrong. In this realm, there are Isaacs and there are Ishmaels. The former are what the Lord has truly done by His power, but the latter are actually us trying to "help the Lord" (?!?) to make a sign or wonder become manifest. Methinks we got enough Ishmaels in this world already that we don't need to add to their number.

No matter what miracle stories arise from this or that sector of Christendom in the earth, I don't seem to be alone in wondering why so many of us who read His Word and say yes and amen to the stories and the lessons about His evident power, that **we don't witness or experience those miracles**. Why is that so?

And so far, I still have no answer for that.

- - - -

We ask ourselves at these moments, "What else could I have done to intervene, to help her, to prevent this kind of heart-breaking tragedy from happening?"

But adult children are gona do what they are gona do. They are no longer seated at my table, no longer living under my roof, no longer required to listen to parents and heed their wishes and directives. And if they choose a path that leads to self destruction, what else can Dad's and Mom's do besides shed tears?

But I have asked for what seems impossible. I said, “Lord, please send Jennifer’s spirit back into her body, and breathe into her again the breath of Life, by Your mercy and Your miracle working power, in Jesus’ name.”

Now I wait.

- - - -

I have been in His presence this afternoon, meditating on a number of miracle stories in His Word. It came to me that we often associate a certain person (other than Jesus) with the responsibility of how and why a certain miracle happened.

“Joshua brought down the walls of Jericho.” No, he didn’t. The Lord did.

“Moses divided the Red Sea.” No, he didn’t. The Lord did.

“Gideon defeated an entire huge army with only 300 men.” No, he didn’t. He was just present nearby when the Lord did that.

“Elijah called down fire to burn up a sacrifice, plus the wood, and the stones, and even the trench full of water.” Ok, fine, he called upon the Lord, and the Lord did the miracle, not Elijah.

I just told the Lord today that I recognize that He alone is the worker of miracles. So I asked Him to work one more for my

Jennifer. “Send her back to us, Lord. Give her another shot at walking by faith in You down here.”

And if that happens, it won’t be because I need or want any credit for such a miracle to transpire. It’s just supposed to be normal, not extraordinary, that miracles happen among God’s people upon the earth. His people in Heaven have no more need of miracles. But we on earth still do.

- - - -

A long time friend and fellow servant in East Texas reached me with the following:

Most of us know we need His evident power all the time. There are probably many reasons why we don’t experience it like the early church. We keep going with Him as you said. It is a wonder Doug Montague has been teaching God’s Word to people all over the world. And it’s a wonder that I have preached and led people to the Lord and baptized them into Christ. Praise His Holy Name! May the Lord continue to do wonders through you and Ruth!

- - - -

Yes, thanks so much for your thoughtful reply, my friend.

Sure, what good would it do if all sorts of miracles happen yet there is no miracle of the new birth taking place? Surely getting saved and born again is the greatest and most important miracle of them all. And I am glad you and I have been included by Heaven in the channeling of that kind of miracle during the years He has seen fit to give us upon this world before we fly away into His glorious presence forever.

- - - -

The Best Gift

I am going through Acts again. Guess what's hitting me this go round? Look at the end of Peter's message on Pentecost when the church gets birthed onto the earth:

And with many other words Peter solemnly testified and kept on exhorting them, saying, "Be saved from this **perverse generation**." (Acts 2:40)

Then turn the page, and look at the end of Peter's message after he and John were used of the Almighty to raise up the lame man to now walk. What does Peter say at that point?

For you first, God raised up His Servant, and sent Him to bless you by turning **every one of you from your wicked ways**. (Acts 3:26)

In both instances, to whom is Peter speaking? Is Peter standing in the chapel at a maximum security prison telling those prisoners who obviously must be vile wicked rapists, robbers, and murderers to turn from their sins to become saved by

Jesus? **No!** Peter is talking both times to crowds of observant, mostly law-abiding Jews who have come to the Temple of God of their own free will to offer worship to the Lord!

Yet that is who Peter means when he calls them to turn away from their perverse generation full of wicked ways. So this begs the question, what is so perverse and wicked in the lives of these people to whom Peter is preaching and urging them to repent? Repent? Repent of… what?

Paul would later write clearly that no one is saved by the works of the Law of God (see Rom. 3:20 and Gal. 2:16). But when anyone allows themselves to believe that he or she can live a good enough life so they need not be concerned when they stand before their Holy Maker to give an account for their lives upon the earth, those very goody two-shoes people are saying, "I don't need help from Jesus or from anyone else to obtain the necessary righteousness to be allowed to enter and dwell forever in Heaven. I can qualify by my own efforts and by my own philosophy to get passed those pearly gates."

Yet those are the perverse and wicked ones in the eyes of their Maker, for they are telling Him, "I don't need the work of Jesus upon His cross to deal with my supposed itsy-bitsy sins in this life. I can be good enough without Jesus to get into Heaven."

Yet as Jesus said on His last night with His men (after Judas Iscariot had already left the room to go betray Jesus to his enemies), "No one comes to the Father (in Heaven) **except through Me**" (John 14:6).

Most folks (probably 90% or more) in this world are not the kind of sinners that we agree are the truly wicked people doing terrible and despicable things to others. For this we can be grateful. Otherwise, this entire world would be *full* of chaos and danger all around us on a daily basis. Paul clarified that there are two kinds of sinners when he wrote the following:

The sins of some men are quite evident, going before them to judgment; for others, their sins follow after. (1 Tim. 5:24)

The people standing before Peter in Acts 2 and 3 were not the kind of sinners who had committed very evident and wicked sins. Yes, there are people in the prisons around the world where those kinds of dangerous men and women are caged like wild tigers. And yes, they too need to hear the gospel message that calls them to repent and get saved in Jesus' name. And thankfully, some of them do get saved.

But most folks in this world are following moralistic guidelines which they just automatically learned by growing up where they started life in this world. All religions contain such teachings.

But the result in their hearts is that they are self-deceived into believing that because they are not rapists, robbers, nor murderers, then that means they are "good people." But their own sins are like the tail on a dog. The tail quietly follows after the entire dog. At times, I wonder if any dog even knows he has a tail until one day while the dog sits, a child comes along and accidentally steps upon the dog's tail. Then revelation hits the dog's mind: yes indeed, I do have a tail.

This is why Jesus taught on the Mount of Olives that even though you haven't physically committed adultery (and thus you were commending yourself that you had not broken that commandment), yet He made His listeners stop and reconsider their own "righteousness" in this matter by revealing that adultery could also be committed in the heart simply by lusting after some other man's beautiful wife (Matt. 5:27, 28). Oops! Maybe we aren't so righteous as we thought we were.

Or how about murder? So you haven't picked up a kitchen knife and plunged it into someone's heart. Very good. But while you are congratulating yourself that you have kept the commandment not to kill, yet Jesus pointed out that your anger alone against someone else is akin to committing murder in your heart and makes you liable for holy judgment (Matt. 5:21, 22). Oh my!

So too in my own case. The way I was raised was by thoughtful and considerate parents who taught my brother and me to become polite and respectful young men. Mark and I learned to say, "Yes sir" or "No ma'am" when talking to adults. We both worked hard to make good grades in school. My brother and I indeed saw bullies in school or in our neighborhood, but we did not join in with their nasty activities. When other kids around us were becoming rebels against authorities, Mark and I remained respectful of such. When the church doors opened for any reason or activity, you could count on the Montague boys to be in earnest attendance.

In short, by all outward appearances, my brother and I were not wicked sinners. So, what were we? We were nice sinners.

Yet the Scriptures do *not* say the following:

"The wages of wicked sinning is death, eternal separation from your Holy Maker; but the wages of just little sinning (you know, like when I cheated in seventh grade math to get an A instead of a B), well, ok, you nice sinners can squeak into the back door of Heaven."

I can tell anyone categorically that such a verse just does *not* appear anywhere in the Holy Scriptures. And believe me, I have scoured The Book many times. That verse does not exist. It simply says, "The wages of sin is death" (Rom. 6:23).

If we take these truths to heart, doesn't it make our salvation all the more precious? Jesus didn't come just to die for the wicked sinners. He also died for me, a rather nice sinner, who was still destined for the Lake of Fire if goody two-shoes Douglas would not repent from my own perverse generation of self-righteous religious people.

As Jesus said rather bluntly, if your righteousness does not *exceed* that of the zealous law-abiding Pharisees, then you will not get into Heaven (Matt. 5:20). What the Scriptures are telling anyone willing to listen is this: **There is no such thing as self-rightousness**. You cannot even find that term in the pages of the Bible.

You can only find it described by Jesus when He spoke of two men who went into the Temple to pray, one being an obvious self-righteous Pharisee *praying thus to himself*, but not really praying to God Almighty. Oh, how proud he was of his supposed righteousness earned through all of his religious works. But Jesus said that such men go home still unjustified in God's eyes. Only the tax collector who worked for the hated Roman government and who was ostracized by his fellow Jews so humbled himself that he would only ask for God's mercy upon himself. He acknowledged himself as a sinner. Jesus said that only this man went home justified, not the Pharisee (Luke 18:9–14).

Righteousness is a gift. That's all it is. You may have received and opened many lovely presents from under a Christmas tree this year. And I hope you thanked the givers of each gift you were given.

But the best gift anyone can ever receive is the gift of righteousness, and it only comes from One Source (2 Cor. 5:21). His name is Jesus, and His righteousness can become ours whether our background is as wicked sinners or as nice sinners if we too will only turn away from our wicked and perverse generation and come humbly to receive that gift from the living Lord Jesus.

Failure Equals Uselessness?

A younger servant from abroad just contacted me out of the blue. I had not encountered him for seven or eight years.

He related that try as he did to maintain and continue in his marriage of five years with his wife, she was persuaded by her father to seek for a divorce, which seems to be on the verge of being granted. She is adamantly opposed to any talk of reconciliation.

You can imagine this pastor's consternation. Not only is his marriage about to end, but church leaders in that denomination's hierarchy are making noises about passing judgment upon him as they may seek to defrock him of his good standing with all those churches.

Here is what arose within my heart to counsel and comfort this brother and fellow servant. I hope you too are blessed:

- - - -

Oh my! So sorry for this news. May the Lord renew your hope that He can and will renew good things into your life in spite of this sad development.

Marriage is a covenant, and every covenant requires both parties to enter that covenant by mutual agreement. But even though it takes two willing people to start a covenant, it only takes one of them to break it. See Jer. 31:32, when the Lord says, "…My covenant **which they (Israel) broke**." God was the faithful partner in that covenant, but His people were the unfaithful ones who caused that covenant to fail.

Yet, in spite of that important distinction about who is at fault when a covenant fails, there are policies set up by denominational leaders at headquarters who pronounce that any pastor who experiences a divorce, irregardless of who is at fault for that failure, gets blackballed from being allowed to continue in ministry within those particular denominations. I imagine that is a dynamic with which you are now wrestling.

What you need to keep in mind, no matter what decisions are made by the hierarchy of any denomination concerning any judgment that they pass upon you in lieu of this imminent divorce, is that His Word also says, "the gifts and the calling of the Lord are without repentance" (Rom. 11:29). So even when mankind tries to deny you continued access to ministry, if you are truly saved and called by Jesus to be one of His servants, then being rejected like a leper due to the stain of divorce that now attaches to you does not mean that the Lord won't open other doors for you to continue to walk out the ministry that He has called you to fulfill before He calls you to your eternal home.

You can also review how things went for one John Mark in Acts 13 and 15. He was a younger saint in the Lord than Barnabas and Paul. When the Lord told the leaders in the Antioch church to set apart Barnabas and Paul for going off on a long missionary journey, John Mark apparently agreed to tag along and learn from these two zealous servants.

But when the realities, pressures, and occasional danger of cross-cultural work began to confront John Mark's senses, he bailed out of his former commitment to faithfully accompany and assist Barnabas and Paul. So John Mark timidly and quickly scooted back to the kind of Christianity and brethren that he was already used to back in Antioch where all was much safer by comparison than on the leading edge of frontier missions, evangelizing and planting churches in the face of frequent opposition and open hostility by stubborn pagans or self-righteous Jews.

By the time you reach the end of Acts 15, Paul turns to Barnabas with a proposal to head out again and go check on how all the new churches they had planted were faring. Barnabas was very agreeable, but he also had a suggestion that they bring along young John Mark on this second missionary journey.

You know what happened. Paul was apoplectic that that particular servant who had failed to complete the first journey should **not** be invited to come with them this time. In short, Paul did not want to extend to John Mark a second chance, but Barnabas was indeed more patient with the younger man.

The reactions of Paul and Barnabas toward a servant with a failure in his life represent Christendom ever since. Paul was not open at that time to agree with Barnabas to give John Mark another chance to serve. Thus, Barnabas took the young man under his wing, and the two of them sailed off one direction while Paul invited Silas to accompany him to go to other areas.

So today, you too will discover who holds a hard-nosed attitude against you so that they will not help you continue in ministry due to how they judge you in these matters that cause you sorrow and distress. But I am glad to report that the Lord still has gentler and more patient servants in His flock who will extend more chances for you to go forward and fulfill the calling that He has given you.

Also there is hope that those who reject you now will someday come around to realize their error of formerly turning their backs upon you, just as Paul did about John Mark. In Paul's last known letter which we call 2 Timothy, what did he say about how John Mark eventually turned out? "Pick up Mark, and bring him with you, **for he is useful to me for service**"

(2 Tim. 4:11). That's the same John Mark whom Paul had brusquely rejected after his youthful failure.

Not only did Barnabas continue to invest himself in John Mark, but later still, Mark also began to accompany Peter. After hearing Peter preach so many stories about what Jesus said and did, one day Mark felt prompted to sit down and compose a gospel account. So to this day, we call it the Gospel according to Mark!

The Lord still makes good use of servants who have failures in their lives, not just before they were saved but even after salvation has begun in their lives. According to Stephen in Acts 7:23–29, Moses somehow already knew at the age of forty that the Lord had chosen Moses to deliver the Hebrews from their bondage to slavery. But he acted prematurely without God's wisdom when he took matters into his own hands and killed a single Egyptian, apparently believing that all the Hebrews would be appreciative and supportive of what he had done, but they did not yet recognize him and his calling. This failure led to Moses' exile who spent forty years away from the Hebrews in the land of Midian.

Yet at age eighty, Moses the failure got reminded at the burning bush that God's calling in Moses' life was without repentance. Moses still had that calling, and now, with his deeper humility in place, Moses was ready to take action back in Egypt according to the wisdom and guidance from the Lord and no longer from his own ideas and imagination.

So keep looking up into the countenance of Jesus, my brother, and try to avoid staring at any angry or hostile faces here below. Their rejection of you for your perceived failures does not cancel out the ongoing providence extended to you from Above. As the Lord manifests good things in you and through you, word will get around, just as it did for John Mark. Then those who earlier figured you to be useless will realize as Paul the aged one did that you are indeed useful in God's Kingdom.

- - - -

Failure Equals Uselessness? (Part 2)

The previous message to that troubled servant has certainly prompted a mixed bag of responses already. That brother himself reports being very blessed and comforted, while some now have a case of the hiccups as they usually try to avoid that subject matter altogether.

But His Word still comes to our rescue, no matter what we face or must wrestle with. My hope is that the Lord will continue to have His way in all of His people's lives. Bon appetit!

- - - -

From that brother:

Very beautiful, pastor, I couldn't hold back my tears while reading to the end. I believe it's God who wanted me to connect with you so that I can receive some relevant and timely counsel, advice, and encouragement from the Word of God itself. 🙏 ✝️

Thank you so much, Pas. Douglas. 

- - - -

Just sent him this follow-up:

You are very welcome, my brother. I am a fellow traveler with you, having preceded you into and through this particular kind of valley. The woman I called "wife" for over thirty years whom I wed when I was almost twenty-three decided three days before what should have been our thirty-first anniversary to pack a bag and abandon both me and our youngest child who was then sixteen with two years yet to finish high school.

She then began in earnest the legal process to obtain a complete divorce, which finally became fully manifest just over two years later. Though she heard from godly sisters who told her what she was doing was wrong and not supported by anything in the Scriptures, she plowed ahead without relenting one iota.

When the divorce got finalized, I calculated the exact amount of time that we had been married as equal to thirty-three years and six days. I thought, *How poetic!* Jesus died at the age of 33 which is when this marriage died, and six days after God created all things, then He rested. So now I too shall enter rest from a marriage that was more like a non-marriage from the start even though I had hoped and prayed and persevered those many years that there would finally manifest a kind of harmony and unity that the Lord intends every marriage covenant to be if the one guideline He gave for who should marry whom has been followed, that is, a truly born-again man is led by Him to find and marry a truly born-again woman. That kind of marriage can be blessed with real unity. Why? Because they are both in the light. Light with light is compatible.

But one who is light trying to unite with one who turns out only to be a pretender, or what the New Testament calls "false brethren" (or what Isaiah calls "false sons"; read Isa. 30:9), means that marriage can never know a successful blending of those two lives since the other partner is actually only darkness. Yes, the two of them can climb into the marriage bed together, and if both are physically healthy, sperm and egg can find each other, and children can be produced. That is a sexual union alone, but not a soul-to-soul union.

Sooner or later, the born-again one will come into revelation from above as to why in heart there is no real oneness between them. Light and darkness do not fellowship. Instead, they mutually repel one another.

If the one in the darkness will not genuinely repent and then become born again, then that dark soul will eventually fulfill what Paul described in 1 Cor. 7, a chapter about marriage and divorce. He says in verse 15 that if the unbelieving half of a marriage chooses to leave that marriage, then the believing half is not compelled to try and keep that spouse within the bounds of that unworking marriage. You cannot force your unsaved spouse to repent and become part of the light.

And at that point, you are ready to trust the Lord to lead you to the saint of His choosing who is truly living and walking in His light. Then the two of you can enter a proper and godly marriage, light with light, born-again spirit with born-again spirit.

- - - -

Here was his next reply:

This is what my ex did to me, almost the same, but mine sooner, just five years; it was like premeditated.

Thank you, God has given you great revelation, and I believe your rich experience speaks right into my soul. I just wanted put it behind me and have already moved on after two years in misery, depression, and almost complete darkness. 🙏

- - - -

My next reply:

I am very glad to be of service to you in these difficult and heart-wrenching matters. Unfortunately, so many leaders in denominational hierarchy just don't want to really dig into His Word and get His full counsel on this distasteful subject.

But the Lord never says "Duh, I don't know" about any topic. His Word is very complete on *all* things.

And as Paul said, "the closer I can become to a man of *all* Scripture, then I will prove myself as an adequate servant (not a perfect servant), able to produce more and more good works" (2 Timothy 3:16 and 17 are called two verses, but in the original Koine Greek, those two verses are only a single sentence, a detail oft overlooked by the saints who often commit 16 to memory but fail to notice its vital connection to verse 17). Together they are a concise and vital unit of truth that His servants everywhere need to notice and then strive constantly to become more and more men of The Book, the whole thing, not just a few favorite stories and a small collection of memorized verses.

- - - -

That brother's next reply:

Well said, pastor, well said. 

We shall talk soon and looking forward to meeting you when you're in Penang.

- - - -

(My concluding cautionary word:

Listen, brother, one more thing.

Maybe you have already tumbled to the following conclusion without my help, but please consider this:

Your marriage and its sad conclusion in this fashion has now shown you what I think many saints have done as they anticipate getting ready mentally for marriage. For whatever reasons, you married without truly being led by His Spirit to try and join yourself to a person not of His choosing.

Now you say, "I just wanted to put it behind me *and have already moved on…*" You may be implying that you want to *quickly* find the next one who says yes to your marriage proposal.

Have you ever heard the expression, "Out of the frying pan, *and into the fire*"? If you don't exercise godly patience at this time, that is exactly what can await you.

Please, brother, slow down in your thoughts. Give room for a renewed time of seeking the Lord, dwelling in His presence, confessing to Him about your former impatience and willfulness to forge ahead to get married when His Spirit was giving you warnings to which you seemed to be deaf. Jesus knows how to open the ears of your heart. Tell the Lord over and over that next time, you surely want to be clearly led by Him in the matter of who should become your suitable helpmate.

Once I gave up hope for reconciliation with the one I now recognized as only a pretend follower of our Lord Jesus, then I began praying and waiting on the Lord for the next sixteen months. Then finally came the day that as the eight-day seminar was concluding in Chengdu where I had taught church leaders more than forty clock hours that I sat down next to a sister who had joined us for the last three days, and I heard in my heart, "Psst, over here" as if I *saw* a gesture toward that woman. That was when the Lord got us introduced to each other.

Then our friendship grew rapidly over the next eleven months while most of that period, we were on opposite sides of the world and making use of looong Skype phone calls twice a day. Our Redeemer gave us to each other, even though to others, it all seemed astounding that He would draw two such different saints together to wed. Yet the one thing that made all the difference in such a positive way is that she truly follows Jesus as Lord, and so do I. That's the only way to make up the threefold cord spoken of in His Word (Eccles. 4:12).

May that become your goal now, my brother. His way and His choice for your mate must be supreme in your heart, as well as His timing.

- - - -

Failure Equals Uselessness? (Part 3)

A pastor friend in Malaysia sent back the following insight after receiving the last two messages regarding failures among His servants:

"Amen! We all go through bitter sweet moments of life and God allows it. Sometimes it's because of foolishness, ignorance, or even greed. We grow wiser through it. At least we are not fools who never learn."

So here is more of my own testimony in this matter that I sent back to him. Hope you are also edified and forewarned:

- - - -

Amen.

I can now look back after the Lord gave me more revelation about seven years ago as to what I did wrong when I was twenty-two and seeking Him for an answer as to whether I should propose to that particular young woman on my campus who was involved in a parachurch ministry called NCF (Nurses Christian Fellowship) to get married or not. I thought there was only two possible answers from Above, which would be either yes or no.

But I was surprised to hear a third answer instead. The Lord only whispered to me three words:

"Love is patient."

Well, yes, that certainly agrees with Scripture, but what did He mean by that reminder?

What the Lord finally got me to realize was that He had not actually given me a Green lite to move forward in that relationship to try and move it up to a more serious level, that is, into engagement unto marriage. I just assumed that if He did not say *no*, and since I really really wanted to get married, then any talk about *patience* simply meant being willing to wait ten months 'til she graduates from college before we would tie the knot.

Now I look back and, unfortunately, can very much identify with the remnant who approached Jeremiah, saying that they wanted a "Word from the Lord" on what they should do next when they had already decided that their course of action should be to pick up everyone and flee off to Egypt. Read Jer. 42 and 43 for that complete story. But the Lord did give an answer through Jeremiah, which was that they were to remain in that land and not be afraid of possible wrath from Nebuchadnezzar. But the remnant didn't want to hear that!

Even today, blessed with the infilling of His Spirit in the New Covenant for every believer, and having been taught about the importance of being "led by His Spirit" (Rom. 8:14), we can still fool ourselves into making our own decisions without input from Above but delude ourselves into thinking that we have indeed been seeking His guidance. In short, we want what we want. So we just want the Lord to give us His stamp of approval to what we have already decided should be our course of action.

On top of that, one could ask me if I was oblivious to certain telltale signs within her life that should have given me pause about the wisdom of trying to take that relationship to that more serious level of engagement. No, I was not oblivious. Yes, I had already seen and heard certain things in her life that should have been heeded as loud alarm bells sounding off.

But I had attained to a certain reputation among my brethren on that campus as being a very zealous and spiritual follower of Jesus as Lord. Now I look back and can understand that I was deafened by that reputation from those alarm bells. Why so? Because I thought I could be "Jesus" for her! Did I consciously think that blasphemous thought? No, I didn't. But now I have reached the solid conviction that **only Jesus can be Jesus in someone else's life**. No one can be a Jesus-substitute for Jesus Himself. Thus, I was doomed to failure by pressing ahead with her.

That marriage failure was not her fault, nor was it God's fault as I allowed myself to think at times since He seemed so passive those many years. But the Lord will not jujitsu anyone into His Kingdom. That failure was my fault completely. And I have now confessed all of this to my Redeemer who has forgiven me and cleansed me from all of that wrong thinking which led to all of that wrong decision-making.

When He told me, "Love is patient," I now see that He just wanted me to be willing to wait on Him. It wasn't time to propose to her. It wasn't His timing for when I should become a husband. But I did not want to wait. I wanted to get married, and I thought that if I proposed, she would say yes, which she did.

So ten months later, we wed and thus began the next thirty-three years of riding the seesaw, with one of us up while the other one was down. The unity and harmony that I craved and longed for never happened. Yet I persevered to believe that if I were patient enough and loving enough and continued to grow in the Lord, that oneness would finally become manifest between us and the fulcrum beneath the seesaw would be destroyed, but instead the fulcrum never crumbled.

Whoever came up with the expression, "Marry in haste, then repent in leisure" surely knew what they were talking about. And my story is a very clear illustration of that truth. But I thank the Lord that He has redeemed my life from the pit while I am still in the land of the living. To Jesus be all the glory!

- - - -

Deliverance from the Mire

Today, Sunday the 22nd, a verse from the Psalms took on fresh meaning for Ruth and I. While being hosted by friends who live in a farm house a few miles outside of Burrton, Kansas, the recent light snowfall had melted, turning the dirt roads nearby into very sticky mud.

Since we left the house to reach the church in town a few minutes after our hosts departed, guess what? I chose the wrong road, which soon became obvious. Oh, it was the right direction but the wrong surface to try and cross over since we don't own a hovercraft. We didn't just slip and slide around. The wheel wells got so loaded up with mud that the tires couldn't spin, and we bogged down. Sigh.

The Psalmist prayed, "Deliver me from the mire, and do not let me sink" (Psalm 69:14). Before making a call for help, I had to determine exactly where we were. That meant I had to trudge 100 feet through muck that tried to suck my shoes off my feet with every step to reach the last sign we had slithered past.

After getting that info, I pulled out my cell and told my host where we were stuck. As I slowly made my way back to our car, my church shoes got heavier and heavier with caked on sludge. Once my bottom hit my seat, I didn't want to deposit a huge load of goo into my side of the car, so I grabbed my ice scraper and went to work to de-mudify said footwear. Ruth wondered if my heart was ok since I was huffing and puffing so much during that tedious task.

Then I looked at my cell again and was surprised to see *no bars* for making calls. How did it work just a few minutes before? Holy Spirit power? Maybe so.

The cavalry was on the way. Folks out here know how to deal with this stuff. One brother got us into his four-wheel drive pickup truck and then handed us over to another brother who awaited on a hard top road fairly nearby, who then whisked Ruth and me off to church where duties awaited.

Then three men got busy connecting a chain to a large farm tractor. That machine in the right hands can indeed force any amount of muck into submission. After dragging our Camry back to the last intersection, it was drivable, sort of, while still having wheel wells overflowing with all of that sticky stuff. That brother made it to the local fire station. He then labored forty-five minutes with a high pressure water hose to de-mudify our pitiful looking car.

Instead of joining the adult Sunday school class that was in progress, I labored in the men's room for twenty minutes, trying to rediscover my almost unrecognizable pair of shoes. Finally, they re-emerged so that I didn't have to bring the message in my sock feet alone.

So the Lord delivered us from the mire and did not let us sink. The church also paid the farmer for his diesel fuel that he used to haul us out of our dilemma, and then they also filled our gas tank. "Thank you, Lord, for generous brethren, who were eager to help us."

But there's another kind of mire called bureaucracy. Ruth and I have been waiting and wondering since she passed the citizenship exam last November 7th when she would be given a date and time for her swearing in ceremony. My dad's joke comes to mind: "For God so loved the world that He did *not* send a committee."

However, just this afternoon, Ruth checked online about her status with the US Immigration. Guess what? Finally, there is a notice which says that a letter will be mailed to her this next Tuesday which gives the date, time, and location for her to be sworn in as an American citizen! So the Lord has not forgotten us. He will pull us out of the muck of seemingly endless bureaucracy.

Once Ruth gets that step done, then we can apply for her first ever US passport, for which we intend to pay for an expedited processing. After it comes to us, then we must transfer her long-term Visa to dwell with me in Malaysia out of her China passport into the American one. After that is successfully navigated, we will finally be ready to book our air tickets back to Asia.

So stay tuned, my friends. And please keep us lifted up, as in lifted up from the mire so we can continue our service for Jesus, both in the United States while we are here and elsewhere overseas in His timing.

- - - -

Come Together Again!

An old friend has been coping with a very long absence from his wife. As my heart goes out to him, I also felt that he needed some exhortation as to what else the Lord wants him to do besides just wait.

If we want to prove the sincerity of our friendship, then Solomon says, "Faithful are the wounds of a friend" (Prov. 27:6). I trust that my counsel to him will be like unto the wound one receives when a surgeon uses a sharp scalpel to slice open a body and then cut out a tumor to save his life.

- - - -

You know, one thing I so appreciate about the Scriptures is that in matters of hubby and wife relationship, His Word is not obtuse, but rather straightforward and His meaning perfectly clear. When it comes to this topic, we who read His Word with the help of His Spirit to open our minds really do a poor job of playing dumb. "Say what, Lord? What do You really mean in that passage?"

So there is one verse that our sisters in Christ Jesus rarely notice, in my opinion, and also most males called to be leaders are rarely brave enough to touch this verse with a 10-foot pole to publicly teach the body of Christ. What verse would that be? Is it tucked away in those parts of our Bibles that many saints rarely read, such as Leviticus or Ezra or Ezekiel? Nope. It is found in 1 Cor. 11:9, which says simply this:

"…indeed man was not created for the woman's sake, but woman for the man's sake."

To paraphrase and illustrate this truth, His Word is saying, "Adam was not made for Eve, but Eve was made for Adam." So the Lord is making things simple for every married woman. Once a woman becomes a man's wife, her priority is her hubby. Not a job. Not her parents. Not a farm or a piece of property. Not something she inherited. Not her child nor her children or other relatives. No. Instead, a God-fearing woman who has a husband can awaken each day with her primary thought and prayer being, "Lord, how can I be a blessing today to my husband?"

Yet with as minimal knowledge that I have about your wife since you and her wed, it seems to me that what she has lacked in her Christian life is the same thing that is oftentimes missing in so many saints' lives, and that is a proper and godly discipling after getting saved. Where are the older women (not old women) who are obeying Titus 2:3–5 so that these mature sisters in the Lord are taking the younger ones under their wing to teach them the importance of loving their husbands and to be subject to them?

Whenever I hear of married couples having long extended absences from one another, my heart asks if that long time apart from each other is truly justifiable. In some cases, there is a cause that prevents them from usually being together, such as in a time of war and the hubby is in the military. Then because of his duties, he cannot come home for months, maybe even years. Or if a spouse is caught in a foreign land and jailed for doing the Lord's work where man's laws forbid such, then yes, that married couple may have to endure a long time of separation until the Lord sets him or her free.

But as best I can tell, those kinds of causes for long marital separations do not apply to you and your wife. And I know this bothers your heart, too, from what you have shared with me across recent years.

But my question is this: Why does this condition of having a long-distance marriage not bother your wife enough that she will seek the Lord for this to change for the better? How can she arise each morning and ask the Lord for His help to be a blessing to you **when she seems content to dwell continents apart**?

Yes, I am fully aware of all the mess that was foisted upon the entire world three years ago called the Covid epidemic and the arduous restrictions that world governments forced upon almost everyone that restricted international travel and so on.

But long before that ever erupted to disrupt so many lives, there has been a simple saying that most of the world knows, which goes like this:

Where there's a will, there's a way.

Your wife is not showing to you, nor to your son, nor to her extended family in her homeland, much willingness to solve this longstanding absence from you, her husband. I have only heard of all the dynamics that you have tried to implement across several years now to overcome this pitiful situation and to be reunited with your wife and son. But so far, the physical separation continues unabated. Phone calls and texts are a poor substitute for personal presence with one another.

Also I am reminded what Solomon said, which is "An adulteress hunts for the precious life" (Prov. 6:26). The verb in that statement is a very proactive word.

When I think of all the documentaries I have seen about lions, tigers, or hyenas who prey upon other animals for their food, they usually have a common tactic. Those hunters don't usually go after a prey while that animal is with its herd. The hunter has more success and exposes itself to less danger *by going after an animal that is now alone and separated from the protection of the herd.*

As I heard a fellow foreign fisherman say once, "For every Samson, the devil prepares a Delilah." Even though Samson was known for great physical strength, he was one of the weakest men in relation to godly morals. That is how he was captured, blinded, and then enslaved for years.

The marriage bed is to be held in honor, so says Heb. 13:4. Yet how can that gift of God to each married couple be honored when one's spouse is far away and long absent? When there is a good reason for a long absence, the Lord will give sufficient grace to both hubby and wife to endure celibate while they await the day when the Lord will reunite them and restore their marriage bed. But without a truly good reason for being apart for so long, why should we expect His grace to help each partner to remain faithful?

May the Lord be with you in a fresh way today. I hope that your zeal to be reunited with your wife and son will also be blessed with knowledge from Above on what practical steps He has for you to implement. Then the predators that are presently stalking both you and your wife will remain at bay because He has shown you both the way to bring this absence to a *swift* conclusion.

- - - -

Peace Needed, But What Kind?

A sister sent a request to me of her urgent request for prayer. Her grown son is a policeman, and as you can imagine, his work involves dealing with dangerous situations. He recently had to use his firearm and shot someone.

So yes, I have prayed for him but also felt that the following exhortation would be very timely for him to consider if his mother will pass it along to him. Hope you too are blessed:

- - - -

Jesus says that He gives a peace unlike any kind of peace that the world gives.

Peace I leave with you. My peace I give to you; not as the world gives do I give unto you. Let not your heart be troubled, neither let it be afraid. (John 14:27)

So what is the key difference between worldly peace and Jesus' peace? The world says you can only relax and calm down *after* a problem is solved, but not before.

But Jesus had not yet solved our sin problem by becoming the sacrificed Lamb of God quite yet when He spoke these words about His own peace that He was willing to share with His faithful disciples. Jesus has peace to give that is not dependent upon the timing of when problems get resolved. His kind of peace is a steady consistent peace of mind and heart, before trials arise, during the pressures and threats of the trial itself, and after that trial has been endured and solved by His wisdom for us to follow.

But who was not in the room with Jesus when He spoke about His peace? Judas had already left to go betray Jesus to His enemies. Only the faithful disciples (not the perfect disciples; He doesn't have any perfect disciples, just disciples who are still being perfected) heard this lovely promise from Jesus about His peace.

So the question for your son is this: Where are you, brother? In the room with Jesus or not? If you are indeed in the room with Him, then He is willing and ready to impart to you His kind of peace, even before you see all things resolved or inquiries concluded in your favor in the matter of your recent actions taken in the line of your police duties.

- - - -

Pointing to Jesus

Before I hit the bed at midnight last evening, a note from a troubled brother and fellow servant reached me. You have probably heard the concept of standing at the fork in the road. You wonder if you should choose the way toward the right, or would it be better to go down the other way. But some forks are multipronged! My agitated friend listed several possibilities concerning which path he should choose.

He concluded his cry for help with the following:

"I'm concerned about the future, though I know Jer. 29:11–13 by heart. In my mind it's clear, but my heart is very concerned."

I suppose we can all identify with his sentiment. But at moments like this, what any troubled soul needs is more than compassion, mercy, and grace.

If we want to prove ourselves as adequate servants of the Lord, then we must rely upon the Lord to help us give His counsel which will mean that we must speak the truth in love.

We must keep in mind who we are and who we are not. Hope you are blessed and further equipped by my brief reply:

- - - -

My brother,

This is a time for doing the three words that Jesus said every weary soul should do in order to come back into a position of rest, that is,

"Come to Me…" (Matt. 11:28).

If you say, "But Jesus already knows everything that I am facing, what I have been through, how broken my heart is, and how confused my mind is on what to do next," yes, your doctrine is correct, Jesus does know all of that and more besides.

But I am not asking about your doctrine on the omniscience of the Lord. I am asking about your obedience.

Jesus also says to "take My yoke upon you, and learn of Me" (Matt. 11:29). What is a yoke for? It is for harnessing a farm animal to be ready to pull a cart or a plow instead of just meandering wherever that loose animal wants to graze in the meadow. Jesus will direct you where to go next and with whom to enter into labor together. A yoke brings discipline into your life. You need consistency in your daily life to keep listening to Jesus, to follow the gentle urgings of His Spirit in your day-to-day doings.

Your temptation right now is to try and turn me or someone else into the source of true rest for your troubled heart. But no one else, no matter how much they may love you and want to help you, can become a substitute for Jesus Himself in your life at this time.

Jesus has the ministry of binding up broken hearts like yours just now (Isa. 61:1). Jesus is the promised wonderful Counselor (Isa. 9:6). No one else on earth can take Jesus' place in these kinds of ministries to restore the welfare that your soul now needs.

So, go into His presence. Be prepared to be brutally open and honest with Jesus. Tell Him exactly what you think and what you feel.

Why? So that once you have spilled your guts to the Lord, then that makes you ready to hear His voice giving you His answers and wisdom on what to do next. Your honesty is valuable, but it does *not* get the last word. The truth of the Lord gets the last word.

- - - -

His Hand or His Heart?

A longtime friend and fellow servant whose family relocated from South America to Canada replied to the news of Ruth's acquisition yesterday of US citizenship in only two years and four months since we opened that process. They too can identify with someone trying to thread that needle of dealing with complicated bureaucracy to get a desired outcome.

So he reported: "When the Lord is involved, things happen. So, it was for us here. People said that we were dealing with magic."

That prompted my thoughts to send back the following. Hope you too share in our joy and will be encouraged to walk daily close to our Lord Jesus, seeking His heart more than His hand:

- - - -

That sentiment reminds me of Simon the magician in Acts 8. He tagged along with Philip and saw miraculous signs done seemingly by Philip's hands. Yet Philip knew it wasn't his sleight of hand nor his power performing those wonders. Then Simon witnessed the greater "magical powers" of Peter and John and tried to buy his way into such ability. That was the way of his unredeemed mindset. To such folks, God's miracles equate only to man's magic or clever trickery.

Simon's mentality is also seen within Herod who wanted Jesus to entertain that bored king with a show of magical power. But Jesus refused to perform anything in Herod's presence. Why not? Because Jesus did not come to entertain us. Yes, everything Jesus said and did was very, very interesting. But He was not a showman, neither then nor now.

As Ruth and I spend time circulating among Christendom in the United States, we see in some flocks how they carry on. Two days after we landed in Tulsa last fall, it was Sunday, and we had no appointments set up yet to go serve any particular flocks.

So with minimal jet lag symptoms to cope with, we got up and attended a service that was nearby our motel. What awaited us upon entry was a darkened sanctuary like when you walk into a movie theater. A team of musicians and singers were spot lighted on the stage. Various colored lights would also flash off and on. We felt like we were attending a Christian concert. Even when a message came forth, though we did hear true things from his mouth, yet it seemed he was trying to incite moments of cheering and clapping as if this were a political rally.

One of my Dad's sayings which I heard him repeat several times in my childhood was this: "Jesus was accused of many things, but He was never accused of being boring." Yet I don't think what goes on in the midst of Hollywood Christianity is what my Dad had in mind as being wisdom for Jesus' churches.

So yes, if we truly walk with Jesus today, He will give His servants power and authority to perform signs which can be witnessed by our natural sight, just like He did with His original twelve men (Luke 9:1–6). But our walk with the Lord is not supposed to have an emphasis upon our eyes, but rather upon our ears, for "we walk by faith and not by sight" (2 Cor. 5:7). How do we encourage our faith to grow? "Faith comes by hearing, and hearing by the Word of God" (Rom. 10:17).

Our faith in the Lord is not enhanced by spectacles. The many miracles which the Hebrews saw in the days of Moses in Egypt, at the Red Sea, and in the wilderness for forty years had no effect upon their minds and hearts, only upon their bodies and their circumstances. It is not His miracle working power that can change us from grumbling rebellious immature saints into mature children and servants of the Lord. As David revealed when he compared those Hebrews with their leader, the Lord "made known His ways to Moses, and His acts to the sons of Israel" (Psalm 103:7).

Neither Simon the magician nor King Herod are admirable characters within the Scriptures. Their desires to entertain or to be entertained are not worthy traits to emulate.

So let the works of the Lord, whether they be miraculous signs and wonders or His favor and wisdom pushing Ruth's petition to the front of the line to now acquire citizenship as an American in less than two and a half years, inspire us to draw closer to His heart. May we learn more of His ways to have greater intimacy with Jesus and to give Him unending thanks for all of His goodness shown to us every day.

- - - -

Jesus Is Lord over Our Transitions

My distraught brother and fellow servant in Asia reached me once again asking for counsel on what to do next since he seems blocked for now to carry on as a full-time servant in ministry. Here is his most recent plea:

"Pastor, I need a job until a pastoral vocation or ministry vocation opens up. Until then, I will be in a dire financial situation before the start of next month. What can I do besides waiting on God? I'm concerned as the days go by. My reserves are soon running out."

The following is what came to me this morning to pass along to him. Hope you too are blessed:

- - - -

The short answer is, yes, my brother, you need a secular job for now. We all have bills to pay if you are now an adult. And as Paul said, "if anyone will not work, neither let him eat" (II Thess. 3:10).

Just because you have a calling from above to fulfill a certain kind of ministry in the body of Christ does not mean that the Lord is in a hurry to get you launched into those works in a full-time capacity. Please let go of the notion that many of us have held, that is, once you have completed one or two degrees in a Bible school or seminary program, then you are ready to begin a full-time career in the ministry.

Sometimes while I am teaching in various training centers where a door has been opened for me to teach in those places for a day, or three days, or sometimes up to a week, the Lord has shown me something I can do in any language which only needs two words to express in two ways. I write on the board the following:

Bible SCHOOL

And then under this, I write the following:

BIBLE School

Do you acknowledge yourself as a graduate of such? Do you now hold one or two degrees or certificates from such an institution? But frankly, if you examine carefully the various courses which they require all students to attend in their degree programs, very little has anything to do with a serious and deep study of the Scriptures. Oh yes, those institutions are indeed schools. But calling them Bible schools is a serious misnomer.

One of my good buddies, a fellow evangelical, asked me something one day while we travailed through the academic program of a very liberal seminary together. He said, "Do you know that this school was first called 'Brite School of the Bible,' but later the name changed to 'Brite Divinity School'? Do you know what that means?" he asked me with a grin. I played along and said, "No, what does that mean?" He answered, "It means this school used to study the Bible, but now all they do is make candy." (In case you don't get the joke, "Divinity" is the name given to a very sweet candy which is made and enjoyed during the Christmas season in America.)

Now why is this little treatise important in relation to your current circumstances of being prevented from having your needed income arise from full-time ministry and thus being obligated to turn to doing secular work for a time? Because as you perform whatever honest labor that the Lord gives you for now and into the foreseeable future, this will be a time period for the Lord to truly expand your knowledge and understanding of His written Word until He sees you are ready to be released from that secular work and to engage in the ministry to which He has called you.

Keep in mind that your situation in life right now puts you into some very admirable company. According to Stephen in

Acts 7, Moses at the age of forty already knew he had a calling from above to become the deliverer of his fellow Hebrews from their Egyptian bondage in slavery. (See verses 20–29.) How did he know about that calling? We aren't sure. Scripture is silent on that point.

But what did Moses do next after this initial failure and lack of recognition by the Hebrews about his calling? He ran away from his former privileged position who lived in a palace where he had no need to work at all and ended up in a foreign land where he now learned to work every day as a simple shepherd of sheep.

Now those tender hands of Moses developed into rough calloused hands over the next forty years of his life. Moses became so familiar with that kind of life (as would anyone who has worked at a certain kind of job for forty long years) that when he met the Lord anew at the burning bush and heard that the Lord had not forgotten about Moses' calling but was telling him that now the time was right to go back to Egypt to fulfill his ministry, Moses is full of excuses. He argues with the Lord for a chapter and a half! (See Exodus 3 and 4.) He was learning a truth that Paul would later write down, which is "…the gifts and calling of the Lord **are irrevocable**" (Rom. 11:29, NASB).

And what was the key thing Moses had now learned during those forty years? Humility. Only now could our humble God begin to work with and through a humble servant to do great things. So when he was younger and very proud of himself, how many Hebrews left Egypt? Only one. Moses himself had to run away. But when Moses was older and now quite humbled by all he had been through for forty years working as a lowly shepherd, how many Hebrews got left behind in Egypt? Zero!

When I was twenty-five and almost done with a three-year seminary program, ready to graduate with a degree the name of which I disdain (called a "Master of Divinity," which sounds like the holder of such is now in charge of God Himself!), I had to put the normal plans for such graduates on hold. Why so? Because the Lord had clarified during my last year in that program that His calling for me to someday become His servant did not mean what I had long assumed that it meant. I was raised a preacher's kid. So I had thought that His calling meant that I would follow in my father's footsteps and become a pastor over a local church.

But instead, through a series of things, He made clear to me that He would send me to faraway Indonesia to teach His Word. That meant I was slated for foreign mission work!

Once I got over that shock and surrendered to this guidance, the first mission agency that I affiliated with and followed their guidelines for the next four years to prepare for field service abroad counseled me *not* to line up a church job for me to begin my first full-time ministry after graduation from seminary in August of 1980. Instead, they wanted me to wait 'til the December 1980 semi-annual meeting of that agency's board so that I would be ready to then follow the board's next guideline.

This meant I had a gap of three and a half months... to do what? Briefly I tried a job in sales, but after only making one successful sale in which I earned just under a hundred dollars, I realized that wasn't a good fit for me.

My first born was due to make her appearance by the end of September. I certainly had my share of bills to pay. So now what? Would you believe that I got hired to work in a pizza restaurant? Can you make much money from a six- to seven-hour shift in such an establishment? No, not really.

But guess what? Early on, I noticed something. After the boss would close down around 11 pm and then we all did clean up duties, I saw several uncooked large pizzas waiting above the oven. "Hey, Boss, what are you going to do with those raw pizzas up there?" He said that since no one had ordered them, he would just toss them into the trash. So I asked him, "Before you shut down the oven, may I bake those pizzas first to take home?" He said sure thing.

Friend, over the next three months, our fridge in that little apartment was overflowing with pizza and all other food items that were normally destined for the garbage heap. We had so much excess food that I began carrying loads of it to all of my seminary buddies who had not graduated yet and were still nearby. I felt like I had become Robinhood the second, taking food away from the rich restaurant (but I did not steal said food) and giving it away to poor seminarians!

Keep in mind your fellow traveler named Paul. Immediately upon the day of his conversion on the road to Damascus, he also learned that God had called him into ministry and missions. Yes, he gave it a good go right after he got water baptized and filled with His Spirit. But the early church had to recognize pretty quickly that Paul became too hot to handle. So he was sent away into obscurity for several years (Acts 9:30). Paul himself later wrote that this time spent away from full-time ministry lasted three years (Gal. 1:18). Yet he too would have bills to pay. So he fulfilled an honest secular job called tent-making. He even reminded the saints where he had pioneered many new churches of his own example of working hard to support himself instead of relying upon financial support from those churches which probably were not strong enough yet to take on that kind of financial burden (II Thess. 3:6-12).

So there is nothing inherently wrong with the proposition that you, my brother, at this time and juncture of your life, you need to trust the Lord for finding some kind of secular work to fulfill all of your daily obligations and financial responsibilities. For however long Heaven ordains for this period to last, the Lord will still be teaching you many things as you continue to seek Him each day.

As Paul found in his time away, he had some totally wrong ideas and interpretations of various Scriptures which he had already diligently studied when he was an avid student under the rabbi Gamaliel in Jerusalem. Before he repented, he thought those Christians were absolute heretics to believe that Jesus could really be the promised Messiah. Why so? Because the Old Testament clearly stated that "cursed is anyone who hangs on a tree" (Deut. 21:23), and everyone should know that Jesus died while hung upon a wooden cross. So what did Paul have to unlearn and then learn properly? He later wrote of this revelation from Above: "Christ redeemed us from the curse of the Law, having become a curse **for us**, for it is written, 'Cursed is everyone who hangs on a tree'" (Gal. 3:13).

In like manner, there are things which you have *learned* during your seminary days that now need to be unlearned. Your time away from ministry is *not* wasted time. The Lord knows your own mind better than you do. He knows what you hold to which is correct and true. He knows what you still need to learn. And He knows what you think is correct but is in reality quite out in left field and needs to be tremendously tweaked!

Jesus will choose the time and place to reengage you back into full-time ministry. When the resurrected Jesus met with Peter and six others of His disciples after they spent a whole night fishing but caught nothing, after a nice breakfast together, He said to Peter, "Do you love me **more than these**?" There must have been a gesture toward something. These… what? Well, what had they just begun to walk past along the shore of that

Lake? The fishing boats, the nets, and their other tools of the fishing trade.

And Peter's answer is clear: "Yes, Lord, I love You more than my secular profession of fishing." Ahh, well, if so, then I, Jesus, have something else in mind for the rest of your life. Feed My sheep. Tend My lambs (John 21:15–20). And after that day, we cannot find Peter ever again casting his nets to catch fish, but rather to fulfill His calling as a fisher of men in full-time ministry.

Paul as well reached a point where he realized it was time to let go of all secular employment as a tent maker. So, he let it go and then was full-time in the mission work which Heaven had assigned to him (Acts 18:1–5).

Jesus is Lord over all of our transitions in this life, dear brother. So fear not!

- - - -

The Importance of Not Quitting

Did you ever read the funny poem called "Casey at The Bat"? Full of pomp and self-importance, Casey had a reputation as a mighty slugger when it came his turn at bat. Pitchers trembled before the mighty Casey.

But by the end of the poem, what happened? The mighty Casey had this time struck out, and his team lost the game.

But we who serve the Lord Jesus are not playing any game. Our works for Him are for real. As Paul said, we should always abound in the works of the Lord, knowing that our labor is not in vain (1 Cor. 15:58).

Three days ago, thinking we were ready to submit Ruth's particulars to apply for her first ever US passport, we toodled over from Arlington to downtown Dallas to an official passport agency. But after paying a high fee just to park our chariot across the street from that federal building, lo and behold, we were told that we were mistaken about coming there. So they sent us to get her application underway at an Arlington post office. Sigh. Strike one.

Next day, we collected up all of the dox, photos, and fees and headed off to an Arlington post office. Lo and behold, we were told that this was the wrong post office and to drive another mile away to a second post office. So we did. Once there, guess what that clerk told us? Oh, for a first-time applicant, Ruth needed to submit her stuff to the Arlington Courthouse. Sigh. Strike 2.

So yesterday, Friday, we brought everything to submit to that courthouse. But they wanted payment in two money orders, not cash, nor could I use my credit card for payment of two fees to expedite her application. Another trip back to a post office, bought the two money orders, and then headed back to the courthouse.

Finally! All was in order, and they accepted everything, telling us that even with expedited processing, we may need another five to seven weeks before said passport should arrive and two weeks later in a separate mailing, Ruth's Certificate of Citizenship should be returned also.

So, three days in a row, we had to apply what Scripture calls **perseverance**. It is also known as steadfastness. As Paul said, "May the Lord direct your hearts into the love of God, **and into the steadfastness of Christ Jesus**" (II Thess. 3:5).

Mighty Casey struck out. But God's people don't say, "Well, after nine innings, we all just quit and go home." No. We say, "It's my bat and my ball, and we don't go home **until I win!**"

Thanks be to the Lord who gives us perseverance until we get the victory! Hallelujah!

- - - -

Prepared for Success?

After reading a ministry update from a zealous servant who is based in what used to be called "French Indo-China," I felt led to reply to his several points of good news with both rejoicing but also with a question. I hope you too will be blessed to consider these matters.

- - - -

Greetings to you, Pas. A------,

I just read your latest update, and have indeed prayed for those matters which are listed at the end. However there is something implied from the 3 prayer requests at the end of your latest update which are a matter of concern. My question for you, my brother is this:

When you make these trips, **are you prepared for success**?

You gladly report about several new souls having become new followers of Jesus Christ. Great ! But now that you have left that area where the new converts are living, who will take these new believers under their wing to protect and guide them into this new life they just began with Jesus as their Lord? They are babes in Christ Jesus, and babies are both cute **and helpless**! Babies cannot tend to their own needs in any way. They can only cry out when they are hungry or they want to be carried or they have stinky bottoms that need to be cleaned up or whatever is their current need.

So have you given their names and contact particulars to any local church leaders who are already established where those new babes now reside so they can do the necessary follow up care and feeding of those young saints in the Lord?

You asked for prayer for them to "continue to stay in the faith." Yes, that is very important. But faith comes by hearing, and hearing by the Word of God, says Paul in Romans 10:17. So who in your team did you appoint **to stay behind with them to teach them more of His Word every day**?

There is a question that I often ask pastors which on the surface seems simple enough, yet it often befuddles them on how to answer me. Here it is: Hey Pastor, among these folks here (in this flock), **who is your Timothy**?

Everyone knows the name of Timothy. But when I ask, "Who is **your** Timothy?", the concept of having someone be in a relationship with you just like Timothy was in a little brother relationship with his big brother Paul seems completely foreign to so many pastors. Paul discipled regularly various men during all of his travels for the Lord, so that all along his way, once there were new victories of winning souls in a given area, then Paul could commission one of his own disciples to now stay there and oversee the ongoing ministry of a new church set up in that place, and for more teaching of those new converts so they could grow up and no longer be vulnerable little helpless babes in Christ.

I don’t mean to discourage you, my brother. Your heart is in the right place to go out and preach the good news to the lost, to pray for the sick, and to rejoice over those delivered from the oppression of our enemy. But a new convert obtains more than a new singular identity, that being, he or she is now a Christian. That person also gains other terms that are also true about their new identity, such as the new believer is...

a sheep **in the flock** of Jesus as the Shepherd.

a body part **amongst many other body parts** in the body of Christ Jesus.

an adopted child **into the family of God with many brethren** through the blood of Jesus shed for each one.

a part of **the bride** of Christ who is being prepared for her Groom for Jesus to wed her someday.

a soldier **in the army of the Lord** under our supreme commander, King Jesus.

These 5 things all imply that each saint is part of a **plurality**.

One sheep alone is not a flock, and in fact, is likely sooner than later to become lunch for the next hungry wolf who preys upon isolated sheep.

My body has many parts, but those parts only prosper as long as those many parts stay connected to each other through healthy joints, and all of them stay in touch with the Head (Jesus), both to report on their welfare, as well as to receive commands from the Head so they get busy to obey the Head's daily instructions.

What is the status of my finger if there is an accident, and it gets chopped off? Yes, it is still my finger, but now it has no fresh flow of blood into it, nor can it receive any instructions from my head since the nerves connecting it to my brain are now severed. So a body part is of necessity connected to **many other body parts** in order to prosper.

An orphan child can rejoice that someone had mercy upon that little one and brought him or her home and now cares for their every need. But our Lord's mercy is so great that His outreach is not just to find one child to adopt but rather MANY. So that newly adopted child should soon discover that God's house contains a large and growing family of many adopted children. Again, "**children**" is a plural word.

In Scripture, the image of the church being likened unto a bride for Jesus is never equated with just a single Christian.

Church is also a plural term, even at its simplest definition of just "2 or 3 who gather in Jesus' name." Matt. 18: 20. So the gathering of just a few is still different from just one isolated saint.

And a new saint can grow and get trained to become a soldier for the Lord. But one soldier alone does not equate to **an army**. An army is again a plural term. Even Solomon acknowledged that "2 are better than one" when it comes to resisting an enemy. Ecclesiastes 4: 12.

So may I ask you quite sincerely the following question: Have you ever yet asked from Heaven to give you a Timothy?

If not, will you consider doing so now?

I don't mean to say that you must try to call someone else into the ministry. No. According to Hebrews 5:1 and 4, His Word makes clear that the only reason anyone should ever enter the ranks of ministers of any kind is because our Lord reserves the right of calling whom He wills to become one of the 5 kinds of servants found in Ephesians 4:11. Aaron, the brother of Moses, did not become a High Priest because (1) he chose that profession for himself, nor because (2) Moses called his brother to become a High Priest, nor because (3) there was an election amongst multiple candidates as to who should become a High Priest for the Israelites, and Aaron got the most votes of the masses.

No. The only reason that Aaron became a High Priest is because God Almighty chose him for that ministry. So it is not your job, my brother, to try and call someone else into the ministry so that he becomes your future Timothy. The Lord Jesus will call whomever He chooses into each and every ministry.

But once He calls someone, then those folks need help. It's called mentoring. Jesus mentored the men He called to follow Him. Elijah mentored Elisha. Moses mentored Joshua. Paul first was mentored by a mature saint named Ananias soon after Paul got saved and called to become God's servant. Later Barnabas invested himself to give further mentoring to Paul until Paul was mature enough that now he could begin mentoring men like Timothy, Titus, Philemon, and others throughout his earthly ministry and mission work.

So, my brother, I encourage you to ask the Lord to open your eyes to recognize the ones who are currently nearby you who have indeed received a call from above to fulfill some kind of ministry, but those folks still need your help as a mentor. Invite those certain few to accompany you in your ministry travels. Let them know from the beginning that your time of helping them and training them will be temporary and short term, just like the pregnancy of a woman does not last for years, but rather only 9 months. Then that child is viable to be ready to live its life outside the womb for the next many decades of its life.

What I am describing to you may sound new or unique in nature. But in reality, every early church pastor did not have long-term associates beside them (as is often the case these days in Christendom all over) but rather they had short-term Timothy's who were trained in a brief time period to soon be commissioned into their own ministries as new churches were continually being birthed into this earth.

Jesus is the Good Shepherd. How do you know if a shepherd is truly a "good" shepherd. Easy. At the end of a long day, about an hour before sunset, what did good shepherds do? They led their flocks into sheepfolds shaped like a horseshoe which had high walls of piled up rocks, and they began their head count. "96...97...98...99...and... huh? This morning, I had 100, but now, one is missing."

So what does the truly good shepherd do now? He assigns a fellow shepherd to stand at the entrance to guard the 99, and then he goes looking for that valuable single sheep who just now happens to be missing. And once he finds it, he picks it up, and **he restores it to his flock**.

This is one of the most telling characteristics of who is truly a good shepherd as compared to who is just a hireling who tries to get by on doing a minimum amount of work in relation to a flock. If something valuable gets lost, a good shepherd will go find it and then restore it.

Myself and many other servants believe that this is what Jesus, our Good Shepherd, is doing for His flocks worldwide today. He is searching out for this valuable ministry of producing Timothy's which got lost around the 2nd century, and He is finding and restoring this kind of ministry to pastors and missionaries everywhere.

Please prayerfully consider what I am sending you, my brother, because my heart's desire is to help your zealous ministry to become even more fruitful and effective than it has already become. With regular production of mentored Timothy's, then you are prepared for much more success after success in the Lord's work.

www.ingramcontent.com/pod-product-compliance
Ingram Content Group UK Ltd.
Pitfield, Milton Keynes, MK11 3LW, UK
UKHW041831200726
13854UKWH00002BA/991

9 798988 465577